FLEEING FRANCO

FLEEING FRANCO

HOW WALES GAVE SHELTER TO REFUGEE CHILDREN FROM THE BASQUE COUNTRY DURING THE SPANISH CIVIL WAR

HYWEL DAVIES

UNIVERSITY OF WALES PRESS
CARDIFF
2011

www.uwp.co.uk

British Library CiP Data
A catalogue record for this book is available from the British Library.

ISBN 978-0-7083-2336-6
e-ISBN 978-0-7083-2337-3

The publisher acknowledges the financial support of the Welsh Books Council.

Designed by Chris Bell, cbdesign

Printed by CPI Antony Rowe, Chippenham, Wiltshire

FOREWORD

Fleeing Franco is the story of the Basque children who came to Wales during the Spanish Civil War. It is a remarkable chapter in British and, in particular, Welsh history. The Basque government, because of Franco's imposed blockade of the north coast from March 1937, which effectively prevented ships from bringing food to Bilbao, had asked nations to accept children refugees on a temporary basis so they should escape the famine and bombing which was occurring daily. By May, the French had already accepted hundreds of Basque children. However, the British government prevaricated, being reluctant to accept refugees, claming that to do so would violate the non-intervention pact. The turning point was the destruction of Guernica on 24 April: public pressure forced the British government to change its mind. It agreed to accept children on condition that it would not be financially responsible for them.

Almost 4,000 children arrived in Southampton on 23 May 1937 and were accommodated temporarily in a tented camp at North Stoneham. During the summer, these young refugees were dispersed to homes or 'colonies' around Britain. About 230 children were sent to four colonies in Wales: Cambria House in Caerleon, Sketty Park in Swansea, Brechfa in Carmarthenshire and Rooftree in Old Colwyn. In this book, Hywel Davies gives an account of each of these, setting them in their political and social context.

Since the Basque refugees were not provided for by the British government, volunteers had to be found and monies collected to pay for their upkeep. It was a time of great hardship and deprivation, yet the immediate and spontaneous response by people in the mining valleys of Wales to the plight of the Basque children showed an extraordinary degree of human kindness. Their attitude is an example of how a nation that had so little itself gave so much, not only in monetary terms but also in emotional support. The evacuation of the Basque children to Wales united the public on behalf of a cause that seemingly transcended ideology. The humanitarian element was of overriding importance: people from all walks of life and from different political persuasions overcame their natural suspicions to ensure that the children were decently housed, clothed and fed.

The Aid Spain movement was already well established when the children arrived and so people had the opportunity to transform passive into active sympathy, since here in person were the victims of Franco. The children themselves undertook to try to raise money for their upkeep by putting on concerts where they would perform typical Basque dances and songs, and their physical presence at these events enabled the anti-Fascist message to be spread.

The value of this book's contribution to popular understanding of the human conflict of the Spanish Civil War lies in its extensive use of eyewitness accounts by the 'children', now grandparents, who lived through the experience. They are grateful to the Welsh for the welcome they gave them, despite times being hard. One of the 'children' was so unhappy in Spain after being repatriated that he returned to Wales where he lived the rest of his life.

In recent years, many refugees have flocked to Britain but our own age lacks the generosity that was shown to the Basque children by the Welsh. The prevailing attitude towards asylum seekers arriving in the United Kingdom has been one of suspicion and hostility. Public discourse on refugees has been dominated by the description of their flooding to Britain to exploit its supposedly generous benefits system and demands have been voiced for a tighter immigration policy. Xenophobia has reared its head and the refugee is presented as a scrounger, dishonest, illegal, a drain on the nation's resources. *Fleeing Franco* reminds us that in fact very few refugees conform to this negative stereotype. They are ordinary individuals to whom something extraordinary has happened and we who are more fortunate should be more sensitive to their needs. This book is an important addition to work in progress about the Basque children: the Welsh can be proud of their treatment of the young refugees and we can learn much from their humanitarian and generous response.

Natalia Benjamin
Secretary, Basque Children of '37 Association UK

ACKNOWLEDGEMENTS

'If you tolerate this your children will be next.'

This book had its beginning in an intriguing snapshot published in a local newspaper.

The photograph was a remembrance of a chapter in the lives of seventy children who came to Sketty Park in Swansea in the summer of 1937. These youngsters were a share of the 4,000 children who came to this country fleeing Franco. Young exiles, *niños evacuados*, summoned for the camera in an effort to bolster goodwill or to reassure fretting relatives that their loved ones were in safe hands. The image was a celebration of survival and seven decades had not dulled its force.

Pictured were rows of dark-eyed children, dapper in their Sunday best, staring out from a sepia photograph. It was a job to judge the season or location. The lads lurked at the back wearing thick knitted jumpers or hand-me-down jackets while, at the front, little girls sat cross-legged in summer frocks. All were spruced up. Sandals, courtesy of Clarks, shone. The girls' jet black hair, brushed to a lustre, was topped with a bow. Imagine the resolve it took to drill these free spirits into conformity. It was not enough to be well turned out, the pose must be correct. If standing, arms should be at the sides. If sitting, knees should be clasped. At the centre were the *señoritas*. Respectable matrons in solemn black, or young women as vulnerable as the children in their care. Occasionally, one of the group, very brave, might defy convention to place a reassuring hand on the shoulders of a little one. It is not the dispossessed or the downtrodden who are depicted, but decent little kids, playful, vigorous, thoughtful and upright, worthy of understanding and deserving of affection. In a little over eighteen months, for good or ill, all but a handful of the children in this photograph had been sent home.

Since that first image I have seen scores of such photographs from Sketty and from the other settlements in Wales at Brechfa, Caerleon and Old Colwyn. The likenesses are almost interchangeable. For the most part expressions are serious, though a few breach custom to share an intimate grin. Here and there a boy may try too hard to impress with pretend swagger or a heated word with a neighbour. A few children, distant and withdrawn, lower their eyes, but most meet your gaze. You are compelled to look.

The civil war that drove these young people from their homes is an overwhelming and almost incomprehensible tragedy. Perhaps the ideals and hatreds of that era can best be pieced together through a patchwork of recollections. In the course of researching this book I had the immense privilege of talking to several of the *niños*. I only hope I have done justice to their various histories. Alvaro Velasco, Josefina Savery, Paula Felipe, José Armolea and Gerado Álvarez were all extremely helpful and generous with their time. I am also very grateful for the help of Pedro Perez who acted as an intermediary in interviewing his mother Antonia and his Aunt Lola.

Alvaro passed away as this book was being completed. His extraordinary journey from Bilbao to Carmarthen, told in an accent that mingled Basque and Welsh, is the story of exiles everywhere and in all periods. Events in Spain robbed him of much of his youth, but Val, as he was called by everyone, was a man with absolutely no self-pity or bitterness. On the contrary, he felt extreme gratitude towards the people of Wales for the welcome that they had given to an 11-year-old in a foreign land. He was that rare thing, a happy man.

Wales became enmeshed in the Spanish fratricide to an astonishing degree. At a time when whole communities in Wales were living off scraps, the intensity of the support for the Republic and the welcome given to the Basque children reveals a great deal about a particular society in that most radical of decades.

In coming to an understanding of the immense humanity and solidarity of that era I greatly appreciated encouragement from Hywel Francis and Rob Stradling. If I have disagreed at any point with these illustrious academics it does not detract from the high opinion I have for their scholarship. This respect is evident in the brazen way I have ransacked their writings. Any errors or misjudgements are my own.

I have been greatly aided by talking to Alun Emlyn Jones and listening to the recollections of Roy James. I owe thanks to Rosemary Logan who allowed me access to private documents. The chapter on Old Colwyn could not have been written without her. The various archive services also went out of their way to be helpful. I am particularly grateful to David Morris of West Glamorgan and Susan Ellis of Conwy. A special word of gratitude is due to Christine Williams for her insight and advice, to the commissioning editor at University of Wales Press Sarah Lewis for her gentle encouragement and to David Fielding for publishing my original article. Also, my thanks go to Lyn Evans and Ian McCloy who made it possible for me to escape the daily grind for long enough to write this book. I also owe a huge debt to Natalia Benjamin who has guided, cajoled and sustained the project. The Basque Children of '37 Association of which she is secretary has drawn to public attention a remarkable part of our history, an episode that might otherwise have disappeared into obscurity. She is the keeper of the flame.

All illustrations at the beginning of each chapter are by Eusebio Asencor.

This book is dedicated to my wife Christine and my children Rhys, Catrin and Jeremy. Thank you for your endless patience, love and understanding.

CONTENTS

1 AN UNCERTAIN WELCOME

THE SUMMER OF 1937 was for many in Wales a brief interlude of normality. The mood, as reflected in the press, was optimistic, even complacent. Royal tours and sporting success inoculated the public against contagion from a hostile world.

In July, the newly crowned King George VI and Queen Elizabeth were on a royal progress through the country. Their route took them to Newport, Swansea and Cardiff via the mining valleys. Everywhere, they were received by large, enthusiastic crowds. In Aberystwyth, 8,000 young people took part in a gymnastic display for the royal couple. In Caernarfon the king knighted the former lord mayor of Cardiff, Sir Herbert Hiles.

Eight months earlier, another king, Edward VIII, had traipsed through the distressed areas of south Wales on his errand of mercy. After looking at the scarred landscape and gaunt faces, His Majesty had famously declared that 'something must be done'. The new king observed royal protocol better than his brother, never once speaking loud enough to be heard in public.[1]

Throughout July and August there was mounting excitement about Tommy Farr's World Heavyweight title fight against Joe Louis in New York. Farr had become the British and Empire heavyweight champion the previous March and was unbeaten. The 'Tonypandy Terror' flew out to the USA on 14 July to prepare for the bout which was held at the Yankee stadium on 26 August.

Louis won on points but there was no knockout and large sections of the crowd booed the decision. After the fight, Farr, who won $50,000 for the evening, declared: 'I've got plenty of guts, that's old Tommy Farr you know, I'm a Welshman.'[2]

That summer, thanks to their spin bowler Johnnie Clay, Glamorgan County Cricket Club was having its most successful season ever. Clay broke all previous bowling records in a match against Worcestershire at Swansea. Overall, that season he took 176 wickets and became a hero all over Wales.

The outbreak of a Sino-Japanese war, the purges in the Soviet Union and the dreadful menace of Nazi Germany could not quite undermine a yearning for business as usual. There were other pressing matters of concern, disputes closer to home, which jostled for the public's attention.

At the National Eisteddfod, held in Owain Glyndŵr's historic capital of Machynlleth, the adjudicators staged their own revolt. They were unhappy at the appointment as president of Lord Londonderry, a non-Welsh speaker. He resigned and a symbolic empty chair was left on the platform of the 12,000-seat auditorium. At the same festival, the architect Clough Williams Ellis made a passionate plea for someone 'to deliver Wales from destructive insanity', by which he meant that planning regulations should be governed by rules of 'seemliness and good order'.[3]

A. J. Cronin's novel, *The Citadel,* was published that year and went on to sell more copies, more quickly than any other hardback novel that decade. It tells the story of an idealistic young doctor who takes his first job in a Welsh mining town and drew heavily on the years that Cronin spent as a doctor working in Tredegar. Cronin's book, according to a Gallup poll, 'impressed' more people than any book other than the Bible.

The BBC began the Welsh Home Service in 1937, broadcasting an hour a day of nature talks, children's programmes, plays and religious services. The mixture was not popular with every listener. There was much criticism of the amount of jazz music being broadcast. One contributor to a listeners' forum in Swansea described such music as 'an abomination' and advised the BBC 'to sack the saxophonists and pension off the crooners'.

However, such diversions could not keep distant troubles at bay indefinitely. It was becoming increasingly difficult for people to pretend that conflicts in foreign lands were no concern of theirs. By that summer, the rumble of distant thunder from Europe had already begun to intrude on the mood of make-believe. Remarkably, a broad swathe of ordinary men and women across Wales began to identify with a particular side in a struggle in far away Spain that had no direct bearing on their daily lives.

In late July, at almost the same time as the first refugees from Bilbao were being welcomed in Old Colwyn, a contingent of the Hitler Youth movement arrived in nearby Aberdovey. It was the latest stop on a trek from Chester to Cardiff. The boys, 'looking smart and efficient in their dark uniforms with white buttons and Nazi badges', were guests of Rydal school in Colwyn Bay. The aim of their visit, according to one of their number, was to show that they could be 'good pals'.[4]

The same week as seventy-two young Basque refugees were arriving in Carmarthenshire, the chancellor of the Exchequer, Sir John Simon, also visited the county. Needless to say, Sir John did not call at the camp. He had come to speak at the Royal Ivy Bush Hotel in support of a prospective parliamentary candidate but much of his speech was given over to the subject of Spain and a defence of the government's policy of non-intervention. It was a warm July evening and the chancellor was in a self-congratulatory mood:

> Did you not feel a little thrilled? Did you not feel that there was something after all in being a British subject? To know that this country had exercised steady, sober and secure judgement in Spain, (hear, hear). In the end the matter will be settled by the Spanish people themselves, nothing that is imposed upon them from the outside will produce peace.[5]

A year earlier, the European powers had signed an agreement, according to which no country would supply war materials to either side in the Spanish conflict. The foreign secretary, Anthony Eden, likened this policy to 'an improvised safety curtain'. The British government stuck unbendingly to this agreement, even when it became clear that Germany and Italy were brazenly supplying Franco with arms. Eden was candid in his justification for non-intervention, declaring: 'We are doing everything in our power to see that we are not embroiled in this Spanish War.'[6]

There were, of course, critics of the policy. David Lloyd George was vehement in his denunciation:

> The Committee of non-intervention is the greatest and basest fraud and deception ever perpetrated by great nations upon weak people. The fact of the matter is that we have been retreating from one point to the other before dictators until we can retreat no further.[7]

However, what one contemporary observer called the 'polite comedy of non-intervention' had a considerable measure of influential support. The real force behind the policy, argued G. T. Garratt, were men drawn from a very small caste who started out with definite prejudices, 'discreet people, diplomats and officials, who had the ear of the establishment'. In a shifting world Franco represented for them orderly government, property and religion. In a book published early in 1938, shortly after his return from Spain, Garratt wrote:

> This new form of Fascism, is essentially an English variety – not going to the extremes of a Mosley, an exotic product not to be taken seriously. The Fascism of the ultra-Conservative is an insidious growth . . . exploiting to the full the mental laziness and insularity of his countrymen.[8]

The policy of non-intervention resonated with many people in the comfortable classes. As the *Daily Mail* put it, 'the British public no longer interests itself in any wars arising from European quarrels'.[9] Many found a genuine difficulty in understanding the nature of the revolt and were confused by the various cross-currents. To simplify matters, a largely one-sided press was mobilized to supply tendentious stories of atrocities and to divide the Spanish neatly into Reds and anti-Reds. Spain was portrayed as an unfortunate country suffering from some exotic disease. It was as well to isolate it from the rest of the world. 'Non-Intervention', wrote Garratt, 'possibly fitted in with the general temper of many English people.'[10]

Before Parliament broke up for the summer recess in 1937, there had been an unprecedented string of by-elections caused by the creation of new peers. All twelve were won by the government candidates. Having successfully weathered the abdication crisis, Stanley Baldwin, champion of 'masterly inactivity', had left office and a new prime minister was basking in public approval.[11] His name was Neville Chamberlain.

Large sections of the British public had a fervent desire to remain isolated from foreign entanglements. Spain was a distant country, priest-ridden and pitiless. Demands to take sides in its war were resented by those who wished not to be reminded of the looming European foreign crisis. Non-intervention was more than a policy; it was a state of mind.

In Wales, to a far greater extent than in Britain as a whole, there was instinctive sympathy for the Spanish Republic. Support for the policy of non-intervention was slight in the extreme. Franco was regarded with widespread loathing. The tumult in Spain broke out while the coalfields of south Wales were in the grip of a period of intense radicalism. It was a time of heightened political consciousness, unprecedented militancy and periodic industrial unrest. One expression of this growing political radicalism was the sense of solidarity with those engaged in similar, even greater, struggles in other countries. From the very start of the conflict in Spain there had been emphatic support from the south Wales coalfield for the Popular Front government in Spain. This support was largely ideological but it crossed party boundaries and was assiduously fostered by the Communist Party. Spain and class struggle became one and the same. The miners' leader Will Paynter wrote:

> It is not difficult for people suffering deprivation and hunger to find common cause with their own kind in another country. They recognise that their struggles are international in character . . . The Welsh miners have a proud history of internationalism. They have constantly championed the cause of the downtrodden.[12]

Outside the industrial heartlands, at least to begin with, support for the Spanish government had been less intense. In the census of 1931, 42 per cent of the population had declared themselves to be Welsh speaking and amongst this group in particular the strength of the pacifist movement acted as a restraint on full-blown commitment to the Republican cause. Wales has a long familiarity with pacifism, a doctrine going back to the 'apostle of peace' Henry Richard, and beyond. It had its roots in the Nonconformist denominations and had many adherents within Liberalism and Welsh nationalist politics. At the 1937 National Eisteddfod, a new pacifist society, Cymdeithas Heddychwyr Cymru, had been launched. Its leading lights were George Maitland Lloyd Davies, who had briefly served as a Christian Pacifist MP, and Gwynfor Evans, the man who would come to dominate Welsh nationalist politics for a generation, then a 25-year-old student at St John's College, Oxford. The society's manifesto advocated the principled rejection of all wars.[13]

However, the practice of beating swords into ploughshares was on the wane. Confronted by a would-be dictator who was an unashamed nominee of Hitler and Mussolini, Wales shed its near-pacifist traditions. The injustices inflicted by Mola and Franco on the Basque country ate away at any remaining qualms. The victims of fascist aggression were undeniably innocent and the Basque Republic was indisputably democratic. Most ordinary people, as well as the majority of Welsh political, business and academic elite, wholeheartedly embraced the cause of the beleaguered Republic. Moreover, support straddled different political traditions. In the matter of Spain, rural, Nonconformist Wales made common cause with the collectivist, industrialized valleys. A groundswell of righteous anger united in dubious brotherhood everyone from Lloyd George to Will Paynter, Nye Bevan to Lord Davies of Llandinam. Victorian ideals of philanthropy and public works dovetailed with ideological commitment to class struggle. For a time it seemed as though the entire Welsh political class, from the Liberals to the Communists, were hewn from the same seam. Of course, there were some exceptions, some who remained indifferent or ambivalent, even a few who regarded Franco as a gallant Christian gentleman. But, overwhelmingly, the Welsh people understood whose side they were on.

The attitude of His Majesty's government to the carnage being visited on the Basques was essentially one of embarrassment.

Throughout the spring of 1937, the Foreign Office had clung to its policy of 'scrupulous neutrality' and continued to resist requests from groups advocating the evacuation into this country of children from the war zone. Two events in particular had caused this sudden switch in the public mood and undermined British isolationism: the naval blockade of Bilbao and the bombing of Guernica. Together they made it impossible to resist appeals for help. If the blockade convinced many of the absurdity of non-intervention, events in Guernica on 26 April demonstrated the policy's inhumanity. Guernica changed everything. It foreshadowed a new and terrible type of conflict – war fought without limits. Once the astonishing viciousness of the bombing raid became known, the policy of refusing entry to the 'orphans of war' became untenable.

Taking children from a war zone punctured the British government's policy of non-intervention utterly. Accepting refugees was a partisan act that relieved pressure on the Bilbao authorities and provided a propaganda coup for the Republican side. It was wholly exceptional and ran completely against the prevailing political climate.[14] Yet, for a short while, an irresistible human impulse changed the public mood and overwhelmed the government. British public opinion had been sickened by the bombing and it was no longer prepared to dismiss the claims of children fleeing a barbaric onslaught. Leah Manning, an educationalist and social reformer, was in Guernica at the time of the raids. From Bilbao, she forcefully lobbied the British government and, astonishingly, it relented, agreeing to allow a few thousand vulnerable children to enter Britain. It was, says Tom Buchanan, 'a rare triumph for emotive political pressure over expert opinion'.[15]

Amongst the British establishment the sense of urgency did not last. By the autumn, Bilbao had fallen to the Nationalists and the emotional impact of Guernica had begun to wear off. The humanitarian tremor that had unsettled public opinion began to fade and old political priorities reasserted themselves.[16] Here and there voices began to question the wisdom of the whole exercise. But by then Anthony Eden's 'improvised safety curtain' had been raised for just long enough to allow four thousand youngsters to clamber underneath.

2 BROTHERS OF THE BLOOD

Da yw caru gwlad ein hunain. Gwell yw caru'r gread gyfan
(It is good to love one's country.
It is better to love the whole world.)
Elfed

THE WELSH WRITER AND POLITICIAN Ambrose Bebb was probably right when he derided as fanciful the idea that the Welsh and the Basques shared a common ancestry, but David Lloyd George had never been one to allow the literal truth to stand in the way of sentiment.[1] In March 1937, the former wartime leader sprang into action, donating £250 from his own pocket to help finance the *Blackworth*, a freighter loaded with sugar, flour, fruit and dried salt fish bound for blockaded Bilbao. To the quayside at Hull bounded the Welsh Wizard. There on the jetty, shaking his white locks and pumping the skipper, Captain Russell, vigorously by the hand, he declared, 'I too am a Basque, as was General Foch. The Welsh and the Basques are the same race.'[2]

It may be true, as one writer alleged, that by the late 1930s Lloyd George was 'the sarcophagus not the symbol' of Welsh radicalism.[3] Nevertheless, it fell to him to give voice, forcefully and plainly, to the growing sense of solidarity that many in Wales felt with the Basque people, 'an ancient and honoured community'. In a telegram to the Basque leader Aguirre after the attack on Guernica, he expressed his sense of shock at the 'spectacle of children massacred in their homes because of the loyalty of their fathers to freedom'.[4]

The intervention by the Welsh statesman evoked memories for many of an earlier wave of immigration. For the arrival of the

Basque children was not quite without precedent. At the outset of the First World War, Belgium had been overrun by Germany and thousands had fled abroad. The refugees who came to these shores had been warmly received and provided with public maintenance. Comparisons were quickly drawn between Belgium and Wales. These were reinforced in one notable episode when twenty-four Belgian fishing trawlers fled Ostend loaded with victims of war. The fleet arrived in Milford Haven where their passengers, who numbered several hundred, were given sanctuary for the next five years. The event became a folk memory and a monument to the generosity of the people of the town was erected on the harbour front. The unfairness of the attempt by a more powerful aggressor to crush the liberty of a small heroic nation had a particular resonance in Wales. The analogy with the attack on the Basque country a generation later was clear.

Others also stressed the bond between the two peoples. In launching the appeal to the Welsh people to support the Basque children, Lord Davies of Llandinam called the Basques 'fellow countrymen' and laid particular stress on the 'racial ties which bind us to the Basque people'. The novelist, playwright and poet Richard Hughes, friend of Augustus John and sometime drinking partner of Dylan Thomas, observed in a newspaper article that the Basques deserved every hospitality in Wales because they were 'brothers of the blood . . . they have so much in common with the Welsh'.[5] Lady Rhondda, publisher, politician and owner of several collieries, was of the same mind:

> The cause of the Basques will appeal particularly to the Welsh, for just as Wales stands in its mountains to the west of these islands, so stands the Basque country to the west of Spain . . . Both countries have through the centuries preserved their individual and essential independence.[6]

There are, if one cares to look, evident similarities between Euskadi and Cymru. The new autonomous republic, with its banner of red, white and green, had a population of about two and a half million. It was a country of mountains, green valleys and rugged shorelines, but also of 'sweating, sulphurous cities where the skies turn red with the belch of blast furnaces'.[7] For centuries, it had struggled to survive in the shadow of its much more powerful and populous neighbours. It had struggled, too, to keep alive its ancient language, a remarkable tongue which bears no resemblance to that of any other people. The devil is said to have devoted seven years to the study of Basque and to have mastered exactly three words. A nation of great antiquity, the Basques have occupied their corner of Europe for thousands of years. They have never been subdued or expelled. The writer Mark Kurlansky has described them as 'a mythical people, almost an imagined people'.[8] They are a people apart. Fierce defenders of their territory, they have gained a reputation for learning from potential aggressors while never hazarding too much integration. The Romans, the Vikings, the Visigoths and the Moors have each in their turn attempted to subdue the Basques and each has been repelled. From medieval times, Basque communities and provinces were governed by a kind of primitive democracy exercised through the heads of families. Ordinary Basques enjoyed liberties that anticipated the Enlightenment by centuries. Basic laws or *fueros* meant that feudalism and imprisonment without trial were ended amongst Basques long before they disappeared elsewhere in Europe. Nominally integrated into the Spanish state in 1530, the four Basque provinces retained considerable autonomy until the nineteenth century, able to veto laws submitted by the Spanish king with the words 'we obey but we do not comply'.[9]

In a world where minority cultures are encouraged to fade gently into oblivion, it is extraordinary that a people called the Basques, like a people called the Welsh, still inhabit their respective corners of Europe. The country has shown what Kurlansky has called 'a seemingly primitive determination to preserve the tribe'.[10] Against all the odds, the Basque people have managed to preserve a rich vein of culture, devout, egalitarian and based on strong communal values. Music, particularly played on the *txistu* (flute) or *trikitrixa* (small accordion), is central to Basque tradition. Great prominence is also given to poetry and storytelling. The *Bertsolariak* is a competition where participants improvise in accordance with a given metre, a Basque equivalent of the eisteddfod. In the 1890s there was something of a Basque renaissance. New words were minted, a Basque flag designed and a national anthem composed. Basque history was further embroidered to equip a new separatist movement, the Partido Nacionalista Vasco, its motto being 'God and the old laws'.

In the immediate aftermath of Guernica, the American writer Dorothy Thompson wrote a poignant tribute to the Basque people in the *New York Herald Tribune*:

> The Basques are one of the rare peoples of the earth . . . having a beautiful language and literature, beautiful bodies and faces, a people proud, independent and free, whose history is as old as Europe and who, during all the centuries, have minded their own business, tilling the soil and building a domestic architecture of purest design and exquisite proportions.[11]

During the Civil War, the stoicism and courage of the Basque people struck a deep chord around the world. Admiration for the tenacity with which the Basques resisted the Nationalist onslaught ran particularly deep in Wales. In part, this was due to the undoubted reasonableness of their government. The Basques were temperate in their politics and governed themselves with discernible competence. In religion, they were pious while avoiding fanaticism. They were fierce in their own defence, but did not mete out cruelty or exact vengeance. The excesses of war elsewhere were rarely seen in Euskadi. The journalist George Steer, who wrote the article in *The Times* that first brought the ghastly slaughter of Guernica to the attention of the world, summed up this sentiment in his epitaph for the short-lived period of Basque self-rule:

> He [the Basque] is proud too, of the year in which he governed himself, of how he kept order and the church's peace, gave freedom to all consciences, fed the poor, cured the wounded, ran all services of government . . . alone in Spain he showed that he was fit to rule.[12]

Many of the children who came to Wales in 1937 were not from an ethnic Basque background. In the second half of the nineteenth century, the population of the province of Vizcaya nearly doubled and by 1894 about half the population of Bilbao were non-Basques.[13] Their families had come from Galicia, Andalusia or Santander to work in the heavy industries of Vizcaya and they could speak only a few words of the Basque language. Amongst the children exiled in Wales, a brother and sister who did speak together in Basque are rare enough to be the subject of comment.[14] There was a danger, particularly in the cosmopolitan cities, that the cultural and linguistic inheritance of their homeland would be forgotten or scorned as outdated.

In a sense, Franco and Mola revived Basque national consciousness for a new generation. Invaded by land, blockaded by sea and bombed by air, an entire society underwent an experience of profound solidarity. Those who went through that experience, or endured the repression that followed, became Basque almost by baptism. Successive generations embraced Basque identity to prove themselves worthy of the sacrifices made by their forebears.[15]

Whatever the similarities in history, politics and culture between Wales and the Basque country, there was another, more tangible, connection: red and brown haematite. The prosperity of both countries depended to a considerable extent on the daily sailings of ships loaded with iron ore leaving Bilbao for south Wales and the return cargoes of coal. The up-and-coming city of Bilbao with its rising entrepreneurial class had its twin in the city of Cardiff. The historian Gwyn Alf Williams wrote that 'Cardiff and its hinterland were entrenched in Bilbao'.[16]

The hills to the north-west of Bilbao contained some of the richest deposits of iron ore in Spain. For eighty years much of this ore had been exported to south Wales. British capital had flooded into the Basque province of Vizcaya, not only to exploit mineral deposits, but also to fund new railways and expand shipbuilding. In 1873, the Spanish Orconera Iron Ore company had been bought jointly by Krupp steel of Germany and the Dowlais Iron Company, Basque ore replacing ore mined in south Wales, which was becoming depleted and was unsuitable for the new process. In return, high-grade coking coal was sent from Newport or Cardiff to the Basque foundries, the *altos hornos*.[17] In the wake of this traffic in iron ore, a huddle of Spanish-speaking communities established themselves in the port of Cardiff, the steel town of Dowlais and in the coal-mining communities of the Swansea valley. The 'orphans of war' who found their way to Wales in 1937 were by no means the first to make that journey. An earlier generation of Spanish workers was already well established here.

At the time of the Boer war GKN had advertised in the Basque country for skilled men to work in their foundries near Merthyr. The general manager of the Dowlais works, E. P. Martin, visited the Orconera Iron Works in Bilbao to recruit skilled workers. The company, needing workers to replace men who had volunteered for the army, was under the deeply misguided impression that the Spaniards might be more biddable than local labour and could be used to undercut earnings and established work practices. Initially, twelve men came over to work as boilermakers. These first workers were housed in the sheds because no one wanted to give them lodgings; Spaniards were reputed to carry knives. Subsequently, Alphonso Street and King Carlos Street in Dowlais were built and became the centre of a community of dozens of Spanish families.[18]

It was to this community that Maria Fernandez came in 1906. Her story would later become entwined with the lives of those children who fled Franco's Spain when she became the matron of the home in Caerleon. Aged three when she left Bilbao aboard the cargo ship *St Miguel*, she was one of a family of nine brothers and sisters who settled in Dowlais. Maria Fernandez was intensely proud of her Basque origins. In an interview towards the end of her life she spoke about the Basques and the Welsh:

> The Basques are like the Welsh in that they are proud of their ancient language . . . Basques have always been fighting for their independence. Both have a language of their own and the feeling is there. They want to be free, away from the Spanish government completely and I don't think that will ever die out.[19]

The community that shaped Maria had great solidarity. Many embraced ideas of socialism and syndicalism. Strikes were frequent, some lasting as long as six months. At such times, soup kitchens were the only source of food and the support of a closely knit community the only sustenance. There was some intermarriage with Welsh families, but links with Spain, and the Basque country in particular, remained strong and in desperate years many returned home.

Yet, despite a history of political radicalism, the Spanish community in Dowlais was in many ways very traditional, patriarchal and religious. Maria's father was strongly anti-Catholic and she received a secular education, but for many the Church remained a great consolation. When the Republican government was elected in Spain, the community in Dowlais was, according to Mrs Fernandez, 'split down the middle'.[20] There were some fascist sympathizers and arguments within the community were heated and frequent. The loyalties of Maria Fernandez never wavered: 'I was furious when Franco's forces marched in to overthrow the government of Spain. I was not attached to any political party – I did what I did because I had a great dislike of Franco.'

A lockout at Dowlais in 1909 caused some of the Spanish workers to seek work 22 miles away at the newly opened, and appropriately named, International Colliery at Abercraf. This was a much more conventional Welsh community than Dowlais, Welsh speaking, chapel going and paternalistic. Its time-honoured values were challenged by new arrivals who sought work at the new colliery. The Spanish were the largest element in this cosmopolitan influx. They created a neighbourhood of their own, transforming the terrace of The Brooklands into Spanish Row, a colourful and boisterous enclave, alive with the smell of strange foods and the sound of exotic music. The newcomers, it was said, smelt of garlic, drank alcohol, played hurdy-gurdies and sometimes danced in the street. Acceptance and assimilation took time. The Spanish had to endure suspicion and hostility before proving themselves as good workmen and strong trade unionists. It helped that many learned to speak Welsh and that their sons excelled at rugby.[21]

In general, the Spanish newcomers were more politically mature than their Welsh counterparts. Most gave vigorous support to their union, some retained membership of the Spanish Socialist Party. It was the men of Abercraf who took the lead in raising awareness of the repression in Spain that followed the Asturian miners' rising of 1934. The miners' lodges in which they were active agitated for a token strike on behalf of their comrades in Spain. They threw themselves into fund-raising for their homeland. The village of Onllwyn, where many of the Welsh Spaniards worked, gave more per head of population to the Aid Spain movement than any other community in Wales. Everyone, it is said, gave something except the colliery manager.[22]

A terrible twist of fate in 1934 immeasurably strengthened the fraternal bond between miners throughout Wales and their Spanish counterparts. That autumn, 266 men perished in a pit explosion in Gresford near Wrexham. The awful symmetry of that disaster with the brutal suppression of the miners' revolution in Asturias shaped a strong connection in the minds of countless Welsh colliers. It brought home directly to working people across national frontiers that they shared similar hardships and that their struggles had much in common. From that autumn onwards many in Wales came to feel that the cause of the Spanish workers was directly linked with their own fight.[23]

The longest-established Spanish community was centred on the terraced streets immediately behind the Packet pub in the Docklands area of Cardiff. For a generation, this enclave based around George Street had provided home cooking and hospitality to seafarers arriving at Cardiff docks on one of the regular sailings from Bilbao. By 1937, it had grown into the hub of a thriving Spanish community of between fifty and sixty families. Here, and in neighbouring Stuart Street, were located Spanish eating places, bars and lodging houses. It was in this street that Santiago Isidoro ran his ships' chandler business and Josephina Perez had her general store and bakery. There were restaurants serving traditional Basque salt-fish dishes, and shops where you could buy Spanish bread, wine, oil and vegetables.[24]

In nearby West Bute Street there was a clandestine meeting point for the Republican cause, a cafe kept by Pepita Campos. It is said that it was to Pepita's cafe that a ship's steward called Ben Evans would come in order to leave and pick up messages sent between Basque children in south Wales and their parents in Bilbao. Evans was working on the Constant Brothers' shipping line, which had resumed sailings to Spain. He would regularly collect packets left in the gentlemen's toilet and then carry them on board ship to Bilbao. This precious correspondence would then be passed to an undercover contact in the city, reputedly a parish priest.[25]

The presence of thriving Hispanic communities brought home to many in Wales the immediacy of the growing crisis in Spain. At the same time, for the children evacuated to Wales, visits to their fellow countrymen do seem to have increased general awareness of the ties between the two countries. The Spanish neighbourhoods became vital reservoirs of support for the International Brigade and for the Basque refugees. Voluntary helpers and interpreters were often drawn from these communities. Frank Zamora from Abercraf was one of three Welsh Spaniards to fight and die as members of the International Brigade.[26] His father became the 'whipper-in' of the boys from the Brechfa colony. Victoriano Esteban, who was killed at Teruel, had acted as translator at the opening of the Caerleon colony. Several of the children were 'adopted' by Spanish-Welsh families.[27] Food from Spanish grocers in Cardiff's Docklands nourished the young refugees. 'Even during the war', recalls Josefina Álvarez, 'we ate very well.' Regular visits to play games of football in Abercraf or sing concerts in Dowlais provided a chance for the children to be among their own people.

By 1937, the iron ore from Vizcaya was indispensable to Welsh steel mills working twenty-four-hour shifts as part of the drive for rearmament. As Nationalist forces advanced on Bilbao, the *Daily Mail* dutifully reported that Franco's troops had captured two lead and tin works, 'thereby saving them from being blown up by the Reds'.[28] This military success allowed Franco to order the resumption of exports of iron ore to Wales. It is a strange quirk of fate that in the summer of 1937 Welsh steel production was being kept alive courtesy of the Generalissimo, while tin plate workers in Llanelli were making weekly contributions to sustain victims of fascist aggression.

For the young exiles making the first bewildering train journey from Southampton to their new homes in south Wales, the landscape must have provided reassurance of a sort. As they crossed under the Severn, the neat English countryside gave way to blackened hills strewn with coal mines. The huge furnaces at Port Talbot, massive chimneys billowing smoke and the profusion of railway wagons were reminders for many of the *altos hornos* and the industrial conurbation they had so recently left. Here was evidence of the vital trade of coal and iron between south Wales and Bilbao, an umbilical cord that had linked the two countries for over fifty years, and had produced a clump of Spanish-Welsh communities. Some already knew that their journey would take them to a country with a distinct language and ancient traditions of its own. Their experiences in Euskadi had schooled them well in recognizing such distinctions. There was, too, an awareness of the strong strain of Welsh internationalism, of the warmth of the support from working people for the achievements of the Spanish Republic. More than one young refugee was told: 'You are lucky to go to Wales.'[29]

The evacuated children are your children. A 1937 lithograph
by the Catalan artist Enric Cluselles. A brother places a
protective arm around his sister while in the background
a city burns. Courtesy of the Ministrio de Cultura, Madrid.

Caerleon was the most successful of the four Welsh colonies. Its financial security was secured through an endless round of fund-raising by its troupe of dancers and singers (*top left*). Vital support also came from the leadership of the South Wales Miners (*bottom left*) and civic leaders such as the mayor of Newport (*above*).

Cambria House opened its doors in July 1937 and was home to fifty-six youngsters. In this place of refuge, young lives were restored to some sort of normality.

This happy photograph (above) from Cambria House masks a sad reality. The children seem at ease, yet precious few had been spared personal experience of tragedy.

Cambria House boasted a mighty football team (*below*) known variously as España Libre, the Basque Boys, the Basque Untouchables or the Basque Wonder Team.

The children who were sent to Swansea were fortunate to be housed in a large Regency mansion set in its own grounds (below).

Mr Saunders in a playful mood surrounded by some of the girls and female staff in the grounds of Sketty Park House. Antonia Lapera is kneeling in the second row.

Acherri, an Alsatian dog, was a gift from a Basque sea captain. He was fussed over by the children and became the mascot of the home.

A snapshot of the señoritas who ran Sketty, together with some of the younger children.

D. Ivor Saunders was the borough surveyor and also the driving force behind the Sketty colony. His family took in a refugee named Aurelia for eight months.

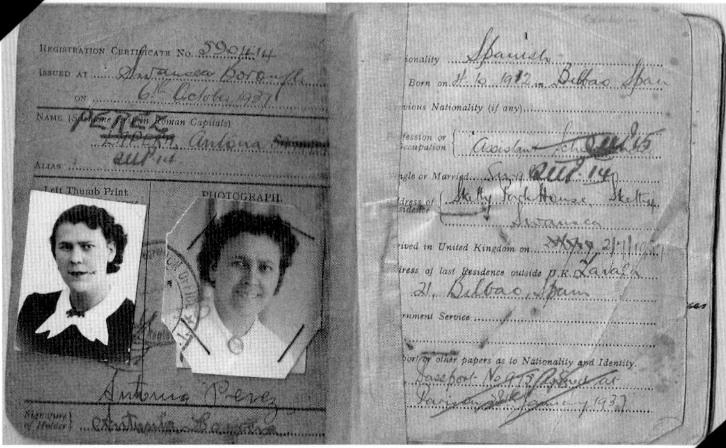

REGISTRATION CERTIFICATE No. 590414

ISSUED AT Swansea Borough

ON 6th October 1937

NAME (Surname first in Roman Capitals) PEREZ LAPERA Antonia

ALIAS

Left Thumb Print

PHOTOGRAPH.

Antonia Perez

Signature of Holder Antonia Lapera

1

Nationality Spanish

Born on 4.10.1912 in Bilbao Spain

Previous Nationality (if any)

Profession or Occupation Assistant School[illegible]

Single or Married Single

Address of Residence Sketty Park House, Sketty, Swansea

Arrived in United Kingdom on 2/7/1937

Address of last Residence outside U.K. Zabala 21, Bilbao, Spain

Government Service

Passport or other papers as to Nationality and Identity. Passport No [illegible] issued at Paris on [illegible] January 1937

The identity card of Antonia Lapera traces her story from Bilbao to Sketty Park House in 1937.

ENDORSEMENTS

Sketty Park House
Sketty
Swansea

Swansea Borough Police
6 OCT 1937
Aliens Registration Dept.

Permitted to land at Southampton on the 2nd July 1937 on condition that the holder does not remain in the United Kingdom later than 2[illegible] August 1937

The condition attached to the grant of leave to land is hereby varied so as to require departure from the United Ki[illegible] not later than 23rd November 1937.

3

ENDORSEMENTS AND REMARKS.

The condition attached to the grant of leave to land is hereby varied so as to require departure from the United Kingdom not later than 25th April 1938.

Swansea Borough Police
20 JAN 1938
Aliens Registration Dept.

ALIENS' REGISTRATION DEPT.
POLICE OFFICE
18 JUN 1938
BIRKENHEAD.

Reports change of address to "Greenbank" Upton on 15/6/38.

Permission to stay in Britain was granted strictly on a temporary basis. Antonia renewed her right to remain three times in 1937 and 1938.

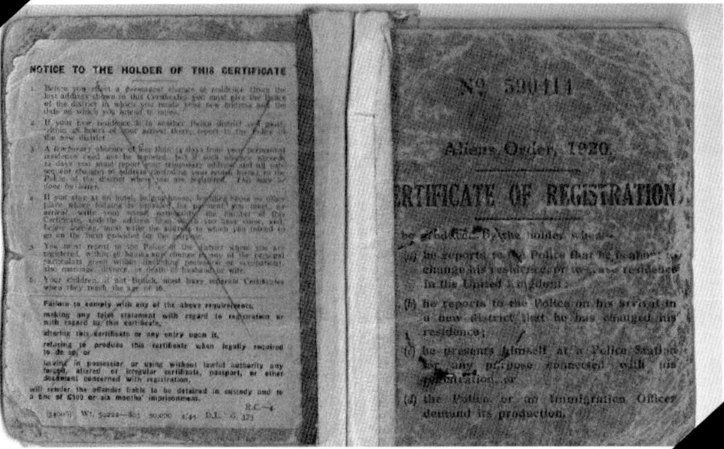
NOTICE TO THE HOLDER OF THIS CERTIFICATE

Failure to comply with any of the above requirements, making any false statement with regard to registration or with regard to this certificate, altering this certificate or any entry upon it, refusing to produce this certificate when legally required to do so, or having in possession or using without lawful authority any forged, altered or irregular certificate, passport, or other document concerned with registration, will render the offender liable to be detained in custody and to a fine of £100 or six months' imprisonment.

Aliens Order, 1920.

CERTIFICATE OF REGISTRATION

To be produced by the holder when—
(a) he reports to the Police that he is about to change his residence or ... residence in the United Kingdom;
(b) he reports to the Police on his arrival in a new district that he has changed his residence;
(c) he presents himself at a Police Station for any purpose connected with his registration, or
(d) the Police or an Immigration Officer demand its production.

ssued under the Aliens Act of 1920, the card had to be carried
t all times and obliged the holder to inform the police of each
hange of residence.

4

ENDORSEMENTS AND REMARKS.

ALIENS' REGISTRATION DEPT. POLICE OFFICE 6 JAN. 1938 BIRKENHEAD.

The condition attached to the grant of leave to land is hereby varied so as to postpone until the 25/10/38 the date on or before which she is required to leave this Country. H.O. GEN 34/4/244

POLICE OFFICE ALIENS 6 AUG. 1938 DEPARTMENT DOUGLAS, ISLE OF MAN

Reported here. Temporary visit.

ALIENS' REGISTRATION DEPT. POLICE OFFICE. 21 JAN 1939 BIRKENHEAD.

Condition attached to grant of leave to land is varied so as to postpone until 25/10/39 the date before which she is to leave U.K. (HO. 2/1/39)

5

ENDORSEMENTS AND REMARKS.

CRIMINAL INVESTIGATION DEPT. 6 APR. 1939 BIRKENHEAD.

ALIENS' REGISTRATION DEPT. POLICE OFFICE. 5 APR. 1939 BIRKENHEAD.

Reports changing her address to Basque Childrens Committee, 4 Great Smith Street, London, on 6/4/39.

HULL CITY POLICE 12 MAY 1939 ALIENS REGISTRATION OFFICE

Reports arrival at "Elm Trees" Church St. Sutton / Hull

Every journey Antonia made was logged: a stay in Birkenhead,

6

ENDORSEMENTS AND REMARKS.

Reported at Mayfield Hotel, Seamer, near Scarborough, on 9/9/39.

NORTH RIDING CONSTABULARY
ALIENS REGISTRATION
16 SEP 1939
DEPARTMENT
WHITBY

J. Nelson
Supt.

NORTH RIDING CONSTABULARY
INSPECTOR'S
13 NOV 1939
OFFICE
FALSGRAVE

Reports leaving Mayfield Hotel, Seamer for London. To be met at King's X by officials of Basque Committee. Address not yet known.

H Craven Inspt.

7

ENDORSEMENTS AND REMARKS.

~~Hotel~~ Changed to.
Northfield
Moor Lane
Maidenhead
Berks.

arrived on
13 Nov. 1939.
reported
9th Jan 1940.
J. Percy Grant

BERKSHIRE CONSTABULARY
9 JAN 1940
COUNTY POLICE STATION
MAIDENHEAD

Until 1940, the Basque Children's Committee remained responsible for Antonia. Officials met her at King's Cross station and from there she began her new life working for the former ambassador.

Rooftree House, in Old Colwyn, was the smallest colony in Wales, with nine boys and eleven girls. The oldest child was twelve years old and the youngest was six.

3 A BADGE OF HONOUR

TO BE WELSH, so the story goes, is to be on the side of the oppressed against the oppressor. Working-class solidarity, internationalism and political radicalism are part of what defines us. They are a fragment of our collective memory, a strand of our DNA. At each juncture of history, when political or social transformation has seemed possible, Wales has thrown in its lot with those advocating change.[1] This thesis has seldom been tested with more rigour than it was in those years following the attempt by a group of army officers to overthrow the legitimate government of Spain. The response of the communities of Wales to the plight of the Spanish Republic has remained part of the Welsh historical landscape ever since. That there was a natural affinity between Welsh working people and 'suffering Spain' has been an article of faith for a generation of Welsh historians.

'The greatest moment of glory was the Spanish Civil War', wrote the eminent Welsh historian Gwyn Alf Williams:

> In a country which had plenty of working-class Spaniards and established links with Bilbao, the Civil War struck an even deeper chord than it did elsewhere . . . To serve in Spain became as much a badge of honour as to have gone to jail for the cause. Lodges raised money, a poverty-stricken people gave milk, money and goods

> to the Spanish Republic and took Basque children into sanctuary, even as Cardiff ship captains tried to run the Franco blockade. Lewis Jones the writer spent his energies on the cause; he dropped dead from exhaustion after addressing over thirty meetings on Spain.[2]

'The issues which were at stake in 1930s Spain, which still concern and fascinate modern historians, are serious, profound, complex, and above all . . . emotional', argues Robert Stradling.[3] But, maybe not – say the tribunes of Welsh history – not in Wales. For the great majority of Welsh people, the Spanish Civil War was not complex at all, on the contrary, it had a beautiful simplicity. Spain was a 'just cause'. The response may have been emotional, but the choice offered was seen as essentially a moral one, between good and evil.

Within weeks of the army revolt in Spain, communities across Wales had been mobilized. River Level Miners' Lodge in Abernant carried a resolution to support Spanish workers and had undertaken a pithead collection less than a fortnight after the uprising. In August, 500 people joined a demonstration in Neath in support of the Republican government. A petition demanding the recall of Parliament to discuss the crisis in Spain was taken from the Rhondda and presented to the prime minister Stanley Baldwin, disturbing his summer break at Gregynog Hall near Newtown. Door-to-door collections took place in every electoral ward in Cardiff and resulted in 11 hundredweight of food and clothing being sent by ship to Spain. In Bedlinog, where half the population was unemployed, the United Front Committee for Spanish Aid collected food and raised £6 in one weekend. By the end of 1936, Spanish Aid Committees were established in Cardiff, Barry, Swansea, Talgarth and in north Wales. The active outpouring of enthusiasm from the working people of Wales for the Second Republic has been well documented, not least by Hywel Francis in his book, *Miners Against Fascism*. 'The depth of solidarity for Republican Spain', wrote Professor Francis, '[was] probably unrivalled elsewhere in Britain'.[4]

Events in Spain dominated the intellectual and political life of Wales to an extraordinary degree. Conditioned by long, bitter years of struggle, the mining communities of south Wales seemed congenitally incapable of staying on the touchline. The supreme expression of this commitment is found in the number of volunteers from Wales who went to fight for the Republican cause: 174 Welshmen fought in Spain, 122 of them miners, the largest regional group in the International Brigade.[5] The various Aid Spain campaigns drew thousands into a mass political movement, a flurry of canvassing, demonstrating, producing leaflets and making door-to-door collections. A new kind of grass-roots campaigning was born. The Basque children who came to Wales in 1937 were the beneficiaries of this period of intense activity.

In his memoirs, the trades unionist, hunger marcher and pithead revolutionary Will Paynter argued that the communities of south Wales had no finer hour than when they responded to the hideous conflict in Spain. It would have been wholly understandable if impoverished people had pleaded that they had other, more pressing, concerns than the repression of liberty overseas. Instead, the war in Spain ignited a most mighty reaction:

> The attack on upon the democratically elected government of Spain produced the greatest spontaneous outburst of popular anti-fascist feeling experienced anywhere. The campaign we conducted for support and aid for Spain and its people was the most responsive that I have ever taken part in; it was magnificent.[6]

But, we have been told, there are no grand narratives any more, no self-evident truths. We seem to have grown weary of large-scale theories of history, be they of class struggle or national identity. Instead, historians adopt a more nuanced, agnostic approach to their studies. Hesitantly, a new breed of academic has begun to expose to scholarly scrutiny some of the consoling certainties that have sustained us for generations.

This process is nowhere more marked than in the study of the role of Wales in supporting the Spanish Republic. In recent years, voices have been raised to suggest that the contribution of our 'small, relatively obscure nation' to the Spanish conflict has perhaps been 'artificially magnified'.[7] Some have asked whether the number of volunteers from Wales who joined the International Brigade was really greater than that from other regions of the British Isles, and questioned whether the support shown for the anti-Franco cause was truly a phenomenon found across the whole of Wales or whether it was confined exclusively to the coalfield and iron towns of the south Wales valleys.[8] Some even suggest tentatively that the volunteers who went from Wales to fight, and sometimes die, on the battlefields of Brunete and Jarama did so for the sake of Stalin rather than for suffering Spain. And, if all this is true, what about that other certainty that lies behind the narrative about Wales and Spain – the belief that there is something distinctive about the Welsh working class. Is our historical memory at fault here as well? Examined more closely, will all the approximations that go to make up national identity crumble into dust? Such questions are, of course, entirely legitimate and, after seventy years, debate is probably overdue. Historical analysis should not be clouded by sentimentality or burdened by ideological baggage. Folklore and myth ought not to masquerade as history.

The welcome given by Welsh communities to the children fleeing Franco is one scrap of a patchwork quilt. It offers partial confirmation that the Welsh response to the Spanish Civil War was indeed as emphatic and inclusive as we remember. At least in the matter of the Basque refugees, Wales showed international solidarity; that much, at least, seems demonstrably true. The children who were exiled here were the physical embodiment of the struggle against fascism. As such, the refugees themselves, and the cause that they personified, were hugely popular with the broad mass of Welsh public opinion. There was an outpouring of popular feeling that was sustained throughout the children's time here. The refugees were met with countless expressions of generosity, humanitarianism and self-sacrifice. Scholarly nit-picking should not be allowed to obscure that reality.

The intensity of the Welsh response to Spain was a product of the distinctive nature of a society forged during the 'locust years' between the wars. It was a time of massively heightened political consciousness, particularly, though not exclusively, in the south Wales valleys. Turmoil overseas, in Spain, Abyssinia, China and Germany, coincided with more than a decade of political and industrial ferment at home. An extra-parliamentary tradition unique in Britain took hold.[9] In the vanguard of this political struggle were various working-class organizations, the greatest of which by far was the South Wales Miners' Federation. Their role was to be absolutely pivotal in sustaining the children's homes in Wales. In addition, the children enjoyed almost universal support from the political, business and academic elite in Wales. The Welsh establishment embraced the cause of 'suffering Spain' wholeheartedly. It is this combination of circumstances that made the cause of the Basque children so special for so many in Wales.

It is particularly remarkable that such levels of support for a struggle overseas came at a time when Wales was itself suffering huge hardship. The 1930s, said W. H. Auden, were the 'low dishonest decade'.[10] Nowhere was the economic devastation of that decade felt more acutely than in the 'distressed areas' of south Wales. The contributions to the various Aid Spain campaigns were made in the face of appalling poverty and levels of unemployment that cut deep into coalfield communities. The people of the valleys were victims of a crisis that was in no way of their making.

There is an apparent paradox here. Unemployment levels in parts of Wales rose beyond 50 per cent. Tens of thousands of families survived on public assistance and the unemployed were subjected to the indignity of the means test. Large numbers of children existed on subsistence diets. Young people left the valleys in search of work. In the face of such calamity, why should people care about what was happening in Spain? The answer was given by a miner who had volunteered to join the International Brigade. Asked why he was going to fight against Franco, he replied succinctly: the Powell Duffryn Coal Company is Fascism.[11]

Lewis Jones's 1939 novel *We Live* is a work of fiction, but it is also a political testament. Jones was a former coalface worker and a political firebrand. By the time his book was published Jones was already dead. He died, it is said, of exhaustion, at the end of a day in which he had addressed over thirty meetings in support of the Spanish Republic. *We Live* tells the story of Len, a Welsh miner who volunteers for the International Brigade. In his final letter home from Spain Len expresses the bond of romantic solidarity that caused men to put their lives on the line on behalf of a distant people and an obscure quarrel: 'This is not a foreign land on which we are fighting. It is home. Those are not strangers who are dying. They are our butties. It is not a war only of nation against nation, but of progress against reaction.'[12] The victims of the 1930s Depression understood the interconnectedness of their struggle with the conflict taking place in Spain. At huge demonstrations against the means test held in July 1936, speakers also denounced the army uprising in Spain. Franco's insurrection was condemned at two huge rallies on 27 July in the Rhondda and in Aberdare. At Neath on 21 August, a crowd of 10,000 was recorded at a demonstration in support of the Republic. The support shown across south Wales for the workers of the Basque country, Catalonia and Madrid was in part an expression of the outrage felt at the unfairness of a system that had also wounded them.

What the poet Idris Davies described as 'the long and lonely self-tuition game' had produced a generation that was remarkably well read and intellectually curious.[13] A consciously proletarian culture was forged, shaped by a sense of shared history and strong collective values. The humiliations and deprivations of mass unemployment sharpened this sense of profound class solidarity; political protest and industrial militancy sustained it and gave it direction. 'Struggle or Starve' was more than a slogan. When the subsistence wage for miners was so shamefully low, when the levels of public assistance had been cut by 10 per cent, when tuberculosis, rickets and malnutrition were commonplace, when there were ten people for each job vacancy and communities were losing a generation through unemployment, self-respect demanded that you organize and express your anger. Part of that anger was channelled into the Hunger Marches which left Wales at regular intervals between 1928 and 1936. Part of it found an outlet in the scuffles with Mosley's blackshirts. Fighting on Spanish battlefields, donating tins of food, or adopting an 'orphan of war' were also expressions of that anger and that idealism.

This was 'a most fruitful period' for the Communist Party in the coalfields.[14] The Labour Party and the official trade union movement remained extremely wary of any industrial militancy, or extra-parliamentary protest. Labour's hierarchy was awaiting the next election and regarded with alarm any association with street agitation, hunger marches or punch-ups with fascists. For many in south Wales, weighed down by horrendous levels of unemployment and suffering from the pitiless means test, such an attitude smacked of timidity. With Labour largely standing above the fray, it was the Communist Party, with a membership in Wales of 3,500, that assiduously gave voice to the concerns of the masses. In 1936, it received its prize when the South Wales Miners' Federation elected the widely respected communist Arthur Horner as its president. In 1934, the Comintern in Moscow had adopted a new, more pragmatic policy of trying to build broad alliances with other parties of the Left. In Spain and in France, this resulted in Popular Front governments, but in Britain, the Labour Party leadership firmly resisted all overtures to join 'unity' campaigns. Nonetheless, at a local level, some Welsh Labour politicians did break ranks to work with communists. In the autumn of 1936, local Labour parties in the coal-mining areas of north-east Wales organized a series of meetings. At one of these, Aneurin Bevan shared the platform with the mineworkers' leader, Arthur Horner.[15] In January 1937 the *Daily Worker* reported six great meetings held to promote 'unity'. The biggest of these at Swansea was addressed by Bevan, Fenner Brockway of the ILP and Harry Pollitt, general secretary of the Communist Party.

The revolt by the rebel generals in Spain produced an unprompted outpouring of solidarity in the Welsh valleys and the Communist Party, which had already established its credibility amongst the unemployed and with rank-and-file miners, was well placed to harness such emotions to its wider purpose. The crusade for Spain became fused with the fight against mass unemployment and offered a new way forward for the party, providing a further opportunity to build a cross-party campaign. Labour, which was officially shackled to the policy of non-intervention by a 1936 conference resolution, continued to resist public campaigns or calls for industrial action on behalf of the Spanish Republic, but it was a position that was becoming increasingly uncomfortable.

The evacuation of the 4,000 children from Bilbao made unity a reality. It offered an opportunity to mobilize public opinion on behalf of a cause that seemingly transcended ideology. People of goodwill from diverse political backgrounds overcame mutual suspicion to ensure that the innocent victims of military aggression were housed, clothed and fed. Communist involvement in providing assistance for the children has been dismissed by some as little more than a cynical sham, Leninists adopting whichever ruse best advanced their final goals. But the unhappy situation of the Basque refugees was not engineered by the communists nor did they orchestrate the intense grass-roots response to the children's troubles. The commitment of men like Will Paynter and Arthur Horner to doing all that could be done to help the Spanish Republic was entirely genuine, but this does not imply that the party abandoned its long-term revolutionary purpose. In the matter of Spain, at least, they saw no contradiction.

Will Paynter, who at the time of Franco's rebellion was temporarily installed as Communist Party organizer for Wales, recalled:

> One of the outstanding features was the readiness of people to give what they could. We could go to the door of any unemployed family in the Rhondda and need only say that we were collecting for Spain and without question or exception we would be handed a tin of milk or a pound of sugar or whatever they had to give, and this week after week from the same houses.[16]

The cause of the Basque children had no greater champion than the South Wales Miners' Federation. The Fed was unwavering in its commitment, guaranteeing the financial security of the colonies in Swansea and Caerleon. The support given by miners in south Wales anticipated by a year a promise made by Will Lawther of the Miners' Federation of Great Britain that 'there is not an orphan child as a result of this struggle who will not be cared for'.[17] The Fed took the leading role in supporting the scores of Basque children who came to south Wales, organizing street collections, donating gifts of food and clothing and securing contributions from every miners' lodge to assure the children that, whatever happened, their needs would be met. 'Raising money from the people of the valleys was never difficult for a cause such as this' wrote Paynter.[18] He showed his own personal commitment to the cause of the Basque children by inviting a 12-year-old Basque girl to come and stay with his family in Pontlottyn. The girl left after a few months to rejoin her mother, a refugee in France. When the Nazis occupied that country, he often wondered what her fate had been. Years later, when he was president of the South Wales Miners, Will Paynter attended a meeting with a research group in Monmouthshire. At the end of the meeting a young woman stayed behind to introduce herself. She was the girl who had been given a home by the Paynter family, she was married and had returned to Wales to live and work.

Any account of Wales's connection with the Spanish Republic runs the risk of self-aggrandisement. The custodians of Welsh radicalism are open to the allegation of distorting the historical record, using an obsession with the Spanish Civil War to inflate the significance of our own small country and, along the way, appropriating solidarity and internationalism as innately Welsh virtues. They are accused of crafting a version of events that validates a particular, romanticized view of Welshness or, in a related charge, of using 'suffering Spain' to shore up a crumbling, collectivist interpretation of the past. In fact, say the sceptics, Wales's contribution to the heroic cause was relatively modest. Interest in the anguish of the Spanish Republic was shallow and fleeting. Wales did her bit, but no more than that, and its commitment was no stronger than that of other comparable regions of Britain. Wales gave her fair share of men to fight on Spanish battlefields; the number of volunteers was about right for the size of the country. Across Britain, various public appeals raised huge sums for the Aid Spain movement, amounts that dwarf the contributions from the radical heartlands of Wales.[19] There was, they assert, no tumult in the terraced streets and little to seize the interest of those with more pressing priorities. The whole campaign was orchestrated by a hard-line cluster of committed revolutionaries with a hidden agenda. Beyond them, involvement was limited to a motley crew of vicars, liberals and the token Tory.[20]

However, incredulity is not the same as insight. Scepticism is not converted into truth by nature of its novelty alone. Certainly, the cause of the Basque children enjoyed broad and deep support in Wales. Their arrival transformed passive sympathy into a real opportunity to do something. It gave a renewed sense of purpose and urgency to an already well-established Aid Spain movement. Here, in flesh and blood, were the victims of Franco's aggression. The children's physical presence at concerts, rallies or football matches offered an opportunity to spread the anti-fascist message to every corner of the country. Their impact was felt in almost every community and for a time they were the focus of a genuinely inclusive political alliance. Time and again, surviving refugees bear witness to the intensity of the welcome they received in Wales. A dwindling band, wrenched from Bilbao and deposited in Brechfa, Caerleon, Old Colwyn, or Sketty, they still speak with deep gratitude about ordinary working families who did so much. Many of those families had themselves been through a multitude of bitter struggles: veterans of lockouts, wage cuts and extreme poverty. Such people did not just sympathize with the Basque children, they identified with them. The welcome given to the children in Wales was propelled by genuine popular feeling. It was that sense of deep-rooted solidarity that gave the Welsh response its 'special quality'.

W. H. Auden wrote: 'I am your choice, your decision: Yes I am Spain.'[21] The decision of the Welsh people in 1937 seems beyond question. Through collective efforts they secured the well-being of hundreds of vulnerable children, despite themselves being mired in poverty. Although the campaign to help the refugees had its heartland in the mining communities of south Wales, it was not confined to those narrow twisting valleys. Indeed, none of the four colonies was actually located in the coalfield. The backbone of the movement was the unions, particularly the Fed, but its reach went far beyond organized labour. It brought into an edgy alliance the revolutionary left and the broad democratic mainstream. It was an expression of gentle humanitarianism and a more muscular commitment to fight fascism worldwide. It was a response shaped by its time and place.

4 THE GREAT AND THE GOOD

On 10 July 1937 Newport railway station was decked out in bunting. The decoration was in anticipation of the arrival of the king and queen on their tour of Wales. On the platform, a large welcoming party was assembled. It consisted of some of the most prominent members of south Wales society: politicians, academics and businessmen. But these luminaries were not gathered there to greet the royal couple. The train that they were expecting had a much less patrician cargo; it was crammed with fifty-two children and assorted helpers. Some of the most eminent men in Wales had turned out to welcome the young Basque refugees who had fled their country six weeks earlier.[1]

To varying degrees, each of the four colonies in Wales that took in Basque children – Caerleon, Swansea, Brechfa and Old Colwyn – enjoyed support and patronage from pillars of public life. For the want of a genuine ruling class, Wales has had to fashion its own proletarian squirearchy, its membership narrow and interconnected. There on the platform, that summer afternoon were several members of this intimate group. Considerable political clout came from Arthur Jenkins, who had worked underground from the age of twelve and served three months in prison for inciting pickets. By 1937, he had risen, via the Sorbonne and Ruskin College Oxford, to become a union leader and MP for Pontypool. That year Arthur's son Roy was studying at University

College Cardiff, a brief stop on the route between Abersychan Grammar School and a glittering political future.[2]

Also on the platform that July evening was the distinguished economist Hilary Marquand. Marquand came from a well-established firm of south Wales shipbrokers and had been educated at Cardiff High School. In 1937, he was professor of industrial relations at the city's university and had just published his influential book, offering ideas to tackle the pernicious levels of unemployment in south Wales.[3] He would later become a Cardiff MP and, for a brief period, minister of health when he replaced Nye Bevan. Marquand's son, David, would also become a Labour MP, resigning in 1977 to work as chief advisor to his mentor, the president of the European Commission, Roy Jenkins.

Perhaps the most significant participant in the welcome ceremony was the shipbroker John Emlyn-Jones. He was a man of real influence in the small, overlapping world of Cardiff society. As a former Liberal MP, he had extensive political contacts.[4] Over many years he had worked closely with Lord Davies of Llandinam, and at one time the two men had planned to launch a newspaper together. He was a good friend of W. G. Howell, who would become lord mayor of Cardiff in 1938. He also had extensive business links through his leading role in organizations like the Cardiff Chamber of Commerce and the Bristol Channel Shipowners' Association. He was on good terms with the principal of University College Cardiff, Frederick Rees, and had family and business links with Marquand. Such a network could be used to support the cause of the Basque refugees. Spain was very dear to Emlyn-Jones. After completing his schooling he had been sent by his father Evan, a coal merchant from Llansawel in Carmarthenshire, to learn business on the continent. He had come back after two years, fluent in French and Spanish. More than this, he returned with an abiding affection for Spain, so much so that he gave his daughter the Spanish name Iñes. Franco's revolt was a threat to the right to 'live and let live', but it was also a struggle for the soul of a country that mattered greatly to him.

From the start Emlyn-Jones made the cause of the Basque refugees his own. He worked with others to ensure that the basic needs of food, shelter and clothing of every child were met. He was a powerhouse who used his organizational skills and his financial muscle to ensure the project at Caerleon got off the ground. His son Alun recalls with pride his father's total commitment to doing the right thing, even at considerable personal cost. He remembers being taken to visit Cambria House by his mother and attending concerts given by the children. He recounts how his family temporarily 'adopted' a refugee of their own. Returning from boarding school in 1937, Alun was introduced to a Basque expatriate who had been given sanctuary in their home in Cyncoed Road. The lad, he recalls, had the whiff of eau de cologne about him. For a 13-year-old schoolboy from Cardiff, such a scent was incredibly exotic. Their Spanish guest stayed with the Emlyn-Jones family until a safe return to Bilbao could be guaranteed.

John Emlyn-Jones's support for the Spanish Republic cost him dearly. Alun estimates that his father lost about two-thirds of his business as a result of his decision to throw his weight behind the Republic. The Cardiff shipbroker had significant commercial interests in Santander and Bilbao. As owner of the Emlyn line, he was engaged in the export of coal and the import of iron ore. It was a lucrative trade which was wrecked by his condemnation of Franco. His involvement with the refugees was prompted by the awkward neutrality adopted by Britain and France after Franco's revolt. Emlyn-Jones had been aghast at the sheer unfairness of non-intervention and felt an obligation to stand up and be counted. He regarded the policy as dishonest and iniquitous and he used his considerable gifts as a public speaker to expose it as a sham. If such campaigning cost his business dearly then so be it. As he told Alun, 'that, my son is the price of principle'.[5]

A young university lecturer called Christopher Hill was also among the reception committee at Newport station. He had arrived in Cardiff the previous October, having been appointed assistant lecturer in history at the university. It was a post he held for two years. From the start, he had taken a leading role in the Aid Spain campaign in the city. By December, the local branch of the National Joint Committee for Spanish Relief had organized the sending of 11 hundredweight of food and clothes to Republican Spain. Such fund-raising evolved naturally into the campaign for the Basque children and Hill was at the centre of a group of students and lecturers who campaigned to bring some of the refugees from the North Stoneham camp to south Wales. As secretary of the Basque Children's Fund in Cardiff, he had attended the meeting on 29 June 1937 of Monmouthshire County Council's Special Committee for Basque Refugee Children. It was at this meeting that the offer of Cambria House in Caerleon as a home for fifty children was accepted.[6] Subsequently, Hill became one of a group of voluntary teachers at Cambria House and took a personal interest in the welfare of many of the children. He was, in the words of Cyril Cule, 'a sincere friend of our cause'.[7]

Christopher Hill was to become arguably the greatest historian of his generation. His radical reinterpretation of the seventeenth century changed the way the English Revolution was perceived.[8] Brilliant and prolific, he achieved his greatest prominence as master of Balliol College, Oxford, a post he held for thirteen years. Hill was a committed Marxist who had joined the Communist Party while an undergraduate. In 1935, he had spent a year in the Soviet Union, a period of his life about which there has been much speculation, particularly since Hill's death in 2003. In the summer of 1937, he was twenty-five years old and had not long returned from Russia. His assistant lectureship at Cardiff was his first academic post.

Also among the representatives from the Monmouthshire, Glamorgan, Cardiff, Newport and Caerleon committees lined up to greet the young evacuees was the principal of University College Cardiff, Professor J. F. Rees. A prominent historian, Frederick Rees was the son of a Milford Haven docker. Both he and his wife Dora were dedicated supporters of the Spanish Republic and as vice-chairman of the Basque Children's Committee in Cardiff, he had lobbied hard to raise funds on behalf of the children and the wider Aid Spain movement. Two weeks after their arrival the children were invited by Mrs Rees to an outdoor tea party on the lawn of University House. Another guest was the duchess of Atholl, the chairman of the Basque Children's Committee, universally referred to as 'the Red Duchess'. She had recently returned from a trip to Bilbao and had witnessed for herself air attacks by the Luftwaffe. At a public meeting that evening in Cardiff's Cory Hall, she officially launched an appeal for weekly or monthly contributions to sustain the children. To coincide with the meeting 10,000 handbills were distributed around Cardiff.[9]

Paula Felipe, one of the children on board the train that afternoon, has clear memories of the throng of people gathered at Newport station. One man in the reception committee she remembers with particular fondness. Cyril Pritchard Cule, the headmaster of Cambria House, still provokes a strong burst of affection: 'Oh he was lovely!' Mr Cule was by all accounts the gentlest of men. He was adored by the children, even if occasionally he had to endure a bit of affectionate mockery. Paula remembers that the girls soon learned to serenade their teacher in English: 'Oh Mr Cule, how I love you, I've got a funny feeling, Mr Cule.'

The son of a Baptist minister from Monmouthshire, Cyril Cule was a romantic, an idealist, internationalist and humanitarian. Steeped in the political ideals of the nineteenth-century Welsh reformer Henry Richard, Cule drew inspiration from the radical traditions of Wales. His commitment to work with the Basque children was explicitly and unambiguously part of a political vision that he outlined in his many articles. In January 1937 he wrote:

> We are already living under a government which, though not openly Fascist, is definitely pro-Fascist . . . We are convinced that the people of Wales are opposed to Fascism, but few people carry their opposition far enough . . . The struggle is the same the world over and the enemy is the same. After Abyssinia, we now have Spain and Euzkadi as sacrifices to international Fascism. Can't we see that the plague is coming nearer?[10]

In 1935, Cule had been an unemployed graduate who had drifted to Paris where he obtained work as a freelance journalist and teacher. Increasingly inspired by events across the border in Spain and the 'remarkable achievements of the Republican government', he obtained a post as university lecturer in Barcelona. From there he went to Madrid and he was in the Spanish capital when the Civil War broke out. His experiences during those tumultuous months left an indelible mark and became the source of his future work as a pamphleteer, campaigner and educator. Spain became Cyril Cule's cause. He wrote that what he saw there convinced him that 'the days of privilege and exploitation are at an end'.[11]

Nevertheless, he did not stay in Spain. At the insistence of the British Embassy, he reluctantly agreed to be evacuated. Joining 1,500 other refugees, he was taken from Valencia to Marseille on board the *HMS Devonshire*. He had considered staying to fight but there was no shortage of raw recruits in Spain and he was realistic about his own limited value as a soldier. His talent was as a journalist. He wrote: 'there is no better service that I can render to the cause than telling my own people the facts as I know them'.[12]

Back in the Rhondda, and outraged at the way the war was being misrepresented in the British and French press, Cule continued to work as a broadcaster, translator and journalist. It was not enough. He tried to get back into Spain as a newspaper correspondent, but was unsuccessful. Then came his chance to do something more for the cause. He received 'a curt note' from someone on behalf of the Cardiff committee: 'Come at once. Teach English.' The newly formed Basque Children's Committee had invited Cule to be acting headmaster of a Spanish school in exile with a weekly wage of 10s. plus board and lodging. His contribution to the success of that school was to be incalculable.

Cule was an active member of Plaid Cymru and, like Saunders Lewis, he accepted that the struggle in Spain provided an inescapable choice. But the choice he made happened to be different from that of the party leader. A fervent Welsh patriot, Cule was also a convinced anti-fascist. In October 1936, he wrote: 'There is room in the party for people like us who are prepared eagerly to accept Communism if we have to choose between it and Fascism.'[13]

An unemployed teacher from Porth became one of Cule's peripatetic staff at Cambria House. Gwyn Thomas had graduated from Oxford the previous year; as part of his degree course, he had studied for some months at the new University of Madrid, where he had wallowed in the writings of Lorca and endured trying times as Spain slid towards civil war. According to his autobiography, he had volunteered for the International Brigade, 'but the local organisers made it plain that the presence of an enfeebled eccentric in a crusading brigade would do nothing but brace Franco'.[14] Thomas, who went on to become a novelist, dramatist and broadcaster of note, was one of a number of university-educated volunteers who taught on an ad hoc basis at the Caerleon colony.[15]

Lord Davies of Llandinam was the Welsh political establishment made flesh. A Liberal Member of Parliament for Montgomeryshire for twenty-three years, he became parliamentary secretary to David Lloyd George in 1916. Uniquely, he had a link with all four colonies in Wales and from the outset he lent his considerable personal prestige and political connections, as well as part of his fortune, to establishing homes for the children. The grandson of David Davies, the renowned Welsh industrialist, he had inherited ownership of Ocean Collieries, a legacy that made him a man of huge personal wealth. He had also inherited a philanthropic conscience that placed him under an obligation to use his riches to advance the common good. There was scarcely a Welsh institution to which Lord Davies did not contribute time and money. He was patron of the National Library of Wales; president of University College Aberystwyth; benefactor of the Wilson chair of international politics; and a generous supporter of the Royal Welsh Agricultural Show. The completion of the Temple of Peace and Health in Cathays, Cardiff, is in large part his project. Its creation was the physical expression of his commitment to the International Crusade for World Peace and the League of Nations Union.

The Welsh Council of the League of Nations was an organization that can justifiably be described as a mass political movement. While it never embraced full-bodied pacifism, the whole purpose of the council was the abolition of international military conflict. It was founded by Lord Davies in 1922 as an expression of the mixture of revulsion and idealism that followed the Great War. He remained its driving force. Its finest hour came in 1935 when, in a remarkable feat of organization, it persuaded more than 62 per cent of the Welsh electorate to participate in the 'peace ballot'. This unofficial referendum was intended to gauge public support for international arbitration, rather than rearmament, as a means of preventing the drift to war. It gives a unique insight into the strength of pacifist sentiment in Wales in those years when an overriding wish to avoid war outweighed a growing realization of the menace posed by Nazi Germany. In short, Lord Davies was one of the great and the good. His initial appeal inspired the colony in Old Colwyn, his defence of the boys who went on the rampage in Brechfa helped calm the fever. His family's donations to the Welsh fund for Basque children, totalling £1,500, put matters in Swansea on a secure footing. Equally importantly, the numerous articles he wrote and speeches he made gave credibility to the appeal for 'suffering Spain', allowing it to rise above ideological differences.[16]

The Basque Children's Committee also included Archie Lush, great friend and constituency agent of Aneurin Bevan. To the great displeasure of the Labour leadership, Bevan had repeatedly appeared on Unity platforms with communists to receive hunger marchers or to resist Mosley's blackshirts. Now he backed the Aid Spain movement to the full, speaking at a large number of meetings in Wales and elsewhere.[17] In January 1938 Bevan made a visit to Spain and on his return declared that the fight to assist Spain must be given precedence over all the other activities of the Labour movement.

The endorsement of so many prominent and respected members of the Welsh establishment is a reflection of the shared assumptions about the nature of society and about the fundamentals of the Spanish conflict. Franco's *pronunciamento* from Las Palmas was met with widespread and immediate abhorrence in Wales. Welsh public opinion rapidly decided that the Spanish Republic was legitimate and heroic. There was little hesitancy, and few attempts to portray non-intervention as anything other than distasteful and dishonourable. Such a consensus did not exist across Offa's Dyke. As the author and politician W. J. Gruffydd put it: 'Wales is such a small country and we all know each other so well.'[18]

5 OUT OF HARM'S WAY

'Si muero, mis hijos se salvaran'
(Even if I die, my children shall be free – Spanish song)

ALVARO VELASCO was taken by his parents to see the king of Spain, Alfonso XIII, as he crossed the border into exile. It is one of his earliest memories. Six years later, Alvaro himself sought refuge in a foreign land. He was one of 4,000 asylum seekers crammed onto a redundant cruise liner which sailed for Southampton in one of the greatest evacuations of children in history. Most of those children eventually returned to live in Spain, but for a few their exile stretched to a lifetime. After many twists and turns, Alvaro came to live in Carmarthen. It was his home for the next sixty years.[1]

Paula Felipe Gomez has her own memories of those wretched and heroic events of seventy years ago. Her journey took her from Bilbao to Caerleon and from there to Skewen where she lives today. She and her sisters, Paquita, Angelita and Rosita, were orphans. Their mother had died when Paula was five years old and her father when she was nine. They lived with an aunt Marcelina and cousins in Portugalete, a suburb of Bilbao. There were seven children to feed and life was far from easy. Paula still does not know who put her name forward for evacuation. It may have been a nun, perhaps it was her older sister Paquita, or it may have been the Basque government – someone had decided that she and her sisters should leave. Seventy years later she remembers: 'boats could go to Russia or England – not a lot of choice. To be honest, the only thing I knew about England was that it was where Lux soap was made. We had a box with it written on the side.'[2]

Josefina Álvarez became a refugee at the age of fourteen. She too was one of the 'brave expeditionary infants' who left Spanish territorial waters in the early hours of 21 May 1937. With her on the voyage was her bother Gerardo, a little boy of seven. It was the first time either had been on a ship. Josefina had been allocated a bunk, but it had been taken and so she spent the voyage on deck amongst sobbing and seasick children. Nearby, Franco's warship the *Admiral Cervera* prowled the waters. Gerardo and Josefina were two of the *Habana*'s cargo of children taken with 4,000 others across the Bay of Biscay to a 36-acre field outside Southampton, to be dispersed from there to a small town outside Newport, a town with a Roman fortress.

Josefina remembers very clearly the moment she felt the first ominous tremors that were to engulf Spain and overwhelm her family. It was July 1936, the summer holidays had just begun and Josefina was fourteen. She had just finished her fourth year at the *instituto* and had successfully completed her end-of-year exams. She did not have a care in the world. She and Gerardo, her younger brother, had their cases packed ready to visit their grandmother. Then, news came that no trains were running. The rebel uprising was more serious than her parents had first thought. The bags remained packed for a few days, but the journey was never made.

Josefina's family had moved to live in the old quarter of Bilbao when she was a young child. Her parents were both qualified teachers. Her mother was a practising Catholic, her father was not. Both were highly cultured, liberal intellectuals who strongly supported the reforms introduced by the Republic, although neither adhered to any particular political faction. Her father's job as an official in the teachers' union would have been enough to condemn him as an enemy of Old Spain. Besides Josefina and Gerardo, there were two other children: a brother aged two and a sister who had already gone to stay with their grandmother and found herself trapped in the Franco zone.

The schools did not open that September, though for a little while the war did not really touch the Álvarez family. Then the bombings started. Josefina's father took the decision that until the tide turned, the two middle children should be evacuated. He was particularly keen that they should go to Britain, which he said was very democratic, very tolerant. It would be twelve years before Josefina could return to Spain. She would never see her father again. When Bilbao fell, he was moved to Santander and after its capture, he was taken prisoner by the rebels and subsequently executed. His last words to his daughter had been: 'Speak English.'[3]

José Armolea was also part of the exodus. He was eleven when he left Spain, and his brother Martín was two years older. José's family lived in Portugalete, about 10 kilometres from Bilbao. His father was a soldier fighting Franco and the rebels and his mother worked as a cook in the town's military hospital. José clearly remembers the dogfights overhead between German and Russian planes and the unremitting air raids which he escaped by taking refuge in a tunnel. His family endured appalling conditions, food was desperately short and even a change of clothes was impossible. Although José's parents were not card-carrying members of a political party, his mother's family were 'politically minded' and his uncle was the town's chief of police, loyal to the legitimate government. The family lived on the left bank of the river and there were frequent bombardments from the opposite side which was under Nationalist control. José was one of four children and the lives of the whole family were in mortal danger.[4]

The desperate choice that faced José's mother and father is beyond normal understanding. To entrust your offspring to strangers at a time of peril goes against every parent's deepest instinct, but the alternative meant continuing to endure a nightmare. A paragraph from Gloria Pilar Totoricaguena's book on the Basque diaspora encapsulates this agonizing dilemma:

> Imagine you are a parent in this situation and you have the choice of keeping your young children with you in danger and harm's way or sending them into unknown exile. In your country, there is lack of shelter, food and medicine. There is a real possibility of political violence. If you send your children away, you do not know with whom they will stay, you could not even chose to which country they will be sent. You cannot go with them. Will

> they be safe with complete strangers? They may forget you and they most likely will resent you. They probably will not speak your language when they return and likely will not have been educated or taken to church to worship in the way you chose. Will you ever see them again? What would you do?[5]

The decision was taken. José and his brother had seen the *Habana* dock a few days earlier. It was at the port of Santurce within walking distance of the family home. Their father was home on leave and he led the way down to the ship. On the way they stopped to say goodbye to their mother at her place of work. It would be their final farewell.

The brutal fratricide that would drive José and the other *niños* into exile was triggered by elections to the *Cortes* on 16 February 1936. The moment it became clear that the Left had emerged victorious, a cluster of senior army officers began to plot the overthrow of the Popular Front government. Their attempted *coup d'état* five months later met fierce resistance and was the signal for a terrible settling of scores that spread like a contagion. Age-old squabbles and dormant hatreds hatched out across Spain. Within days, the entire country was propelled into chaos.

This was no clean war of two Spains, Nationalist and Republican. In the Basque country, as in Catalonia, a longing for liberty transcended the claims of religion or ideology. The Basque autonomous government was made up of devout Catholics, bourgeois liberals who for the most part did not share the revolutionary commitment of other members of the anti-Franco alliance. They threw in their lot with the Popular Front government in Madrid because they knew that Franco would never respect Basque autonomy. In the eyes of the Generalissimo, separatism was not merely mistaken, it was treason. 'Better a Red Spain than a broken Spain', wrote the Falangist politician Calvo Sotelo.[6] The continued existence of a self-governing Basque state (Euskadi) was dependent on the survival of the Spanish Republic and that meant fighting alongside parties with a very different ideological agenda. The fiery Basque president, José Aguirre, himself embodied this incongruity. A pious Catholic who kept a tall ebony and gold crucifix on his desk, his overriding goal was Basque self-government.

Nevertheless, he used the rhetoric of class struggle, condemning capitalism for 'clinging to abuse and privilege' and contrasting this with the 'deep feeling for social justice that is latent in the masses'.[7]

At first, the Basque provinces were left almost alone but in early September General Emilio Mola, the commander of the Nationalist forces in the north, overran Irun near the French border to threaten San Sebastian. Alvaro's family lived in the coastal city where his father was a railway worker. There, they endured the systematic bombardment of their city by Franco's warships. During one dreadful bombing raid on 22 September their home and all the apartments around them were destroyed. Alvaro recalled how, miraculously, the Velasco family survived:

> My sister Margarita, who was pregnant at that time, was in the house, you see. We heard sirens and thank God she moved from the kitchen to the bedroom and in that way she was saved. The front of the house was undamaged, but the back completely destroyed. Our flat had been on the fourth floor and suddenly we realised we were on the second. Ours was the first block in San Sebastian to be bombed.[8]

Having sent an ultimatum that the population of San Sebastian had forty-eight hours to leave before he advanced, Mola entered the city virtually without resistance. Alvaro and his family were among the exodus of refugees fleeing westwards to Bilbao. The population of that city increased from 175,000 to over 400,000 as civilians escaped from an insurgent army that was getting ever closer. The Republican north of Spain was shrinking and resistance was being brushed aside.

For Paula there was no school once the troubles started. The children spent three-quarters of each day in shelters, going down the steps to escape the air raids. During those last weeks in Bilbao, she remembers, there was bombing every day. There was a curfew and shutters had to be closed. The fighting was bad and getting nearer: there were soldiers marching through the city and shouts in the street of '*No pasarán: pasaremos*' (They shall not pass: we shall pass).

Bilbao was the city of sieges. Three times in the previous century it had been surrounded by enemy forces; three times it had resisted the assault. But never before had the odds been stacked so heavily against the defenders and never before had the enemy been prepared to use such tactics. By the spring of 1937, Basque infantry battalions were being pushed back to the 'belt of iron', a network of fortifications, barbed wire and trenches that surrounded their city. Badly armed and poorly trained, their valiant, spur-of-the-moment resistance was severely hampered by the lack of heavy weaponry and the absence of any air defences worthy of the name. Artillery and aerial bombardment had reduced Basque forward positions to rubble. Soldiers marked each day that passed by cutting a notch into the walls of their dugouts as General Mola's units, Spanish, Italian and north African, crept ever closer. But still Bilbao did not fall.

From the outset food had been in short supply. It was a struggle to put a meal on the table. There was tight rationing, and the population survived on almost nothing, eating chickpeas for weeks on end. Paula recalls the hunger that took over her life. Days were spent queuing for bread that was unfit to eat: coarse, black bread made from sweepings, full of bits of string and the occasional nail. She remembers coming home one day to a lovely smell in the kitchen. It was a casserole, a very rare treat because there was not a lot of meat about. At the end of the meal she asked: 'where is the cat for to get rid of that gristle?' It was some time before she grasped the fate that had befallen her family pet.[9]

The desperate plight of the population of Bilbao caught the imagination of the world's press thanks to the media-friendly actions of a handful of sea captains. Three of these skippers were called Jones. To distinguish between them, each was christened with an implausible nickname, becoming Ham and Eggs Jones, Potato Jones and Corn Cob Jones.[10] The authorities in the Basque capital had offered enticing financial rewards of up to 100 per cent profit for cargoes of food, but the Nationalist battleship *España* threatened to sink any ship that dared to enter the harbour.[11] Half a dozen captains of rusty little steamers with cargoes of decaying food remained stranded in the French port of St Jean de Luz. Meanwhile, acting on instructions from the Admiralty, *HMS Hood*, the most potent warship in the world with Vice-Admiral Geoffrey

Blake on its quarterdeck, refused to offer protection to British shipping inside Spanish waters.

Swansea seaman, Captain David (Potato) Jones was part-owner of the *Marie Llewellyn*. In April 1937 he gained worldwide fame for daring to take on Franco's Armada. Thundering, 'has our navy lost its guts?', Potato Jones put out to sea to run the blockade unprotected. For a few days *El Patatero* was hailed as a swashbuckling hero, although the episode ended in farce when he failed to get through and finally landed his cargo in Alicante.[12] Subsequently, there have been claims that this particular humanitarian mission was a cover for gun-running. In his late fifties, David 'Potato' Jones had gone into business with Swansea landlady Edith Scott. They owned three tramp steamers which, it is alleged, were used to run weapons to northern Spain. The accusation is that underneath the cargo of potatoes were guns from Rotterdam. Later, Jones engaged in true heroics when he helped move thousands of refugees from Spain to France.

It was another ship, the Cardiff-registered *Seven Seas Spray*, commanded by Captain William Roberts, which made the first successful dash across the Bay of Biscay to enter the harbour on 19 April 1937. As they docked at the quayside the famished people of Bilbao poured out to cheer Roberts, who was accompanied on the bridge by his teenage daughter Fifi. A banquet was held in their honour and Roberts was presented with a silver cigarette case by the Basque government. The Nationalist naval cordon had been shown to be feeble. Other supply ships rushed to follow the *Seven Seas Spray* and, for a while, the threat of starvation was lifted from the people of Bilbao.[13] The blockade of Bilbao by Nationalist warships had been shown to be porous, but the city remained almost completely surrounded by Mola's army and at the mercy of incessant German aerial bombing raids. In a leaflet drop on the city, Mola had warned the population: 'If submission is not immediate, I will raze Vizcaya to the ground, beginning with the industries of war. I have the means to do so.'[14] The bombings at Durango and Guernica were proof that Emilio Mola was a man of his word.

Guernica is a market town 30 kilometres east of Bilbao. An unremarkable place in most ways, it is nevertheless a site of great historic importance for the Basque people. They made visits there, as if on pilgrimage, to view the 300-year-old petrified trunk of an oak tree, the symbol of their historic liberties. For centuries, as soon as a monarch succeeded to the throne of Spain he, or a representative, had to go to Guernica. There, beneath this oak, where community leaders met in assembly, he swore to uphold Basque laws. On the afternoon of 26 April 1937, Guernica became renowned throughout the world for a reason that went beyond ancient symbolism. It was selected by Lieutenant Colonel Wolfram Richthofen, a cousin of the Red Baron, as the target for a saturation aerial bombardment. In his 1934 book *Die Totale Krieg*, General Erich Ludendorff had argued that modern warfare was all encompassing. No one could or should be spared by the military. Civilians were also combatants and should be treated accordingly. His thesis was tested in Guernica.[15]

With Franco's collusion, an unprotected town, 30 kilometres behind the front line, was attacked by planes from Hitler's Condor Legion. It was Monday, a market day, and Guernica was swollen with people. By the time the planes left, the town was in ruins and hundreds were dead. The exact number is still disputed. No strictly military objectives were touched: factories and bridges were left alone. The planes flew as low as 600 feet and civilians were the only targets. It was not the first place to be mercilessly bombarded in this way. Already, on 31 March, 121 civilians had been killed in a German air raid on another Basque town, Durango. But it was Guernica that was to become shorthand for the barbarity of modern warfare. The butchery had one aim – to terrify those who resisted Franco's advance.[16]

After that, everything happened very quickly. In a radio broadcast President Aguirre pleaded, 'save our women and children, for our men we ask nothing'. The appalling air raids on Durango and Guernica gave warning of the carnage Franco's allies were capable of delivering.[17] The citizens of Bilbao believed that they would be next. Their children's very survival was in doubt. Alvaro's parents made a desperate decision that would change his entire life. They would send their youngest son away to safety, away from the threat of bombing or starvation. Alvaro was the youngest of four children, and ten years separated him from his nearest sibling. His birth after such a long gap made him particularly precious. He had to go, they said, 'so that there will be at least one of us alive'. In hundreds of other homes the same decision was being made.

Parents were convinced that they were sending their loved ones into exile for a short period: 'only for three months'. All had absolute belief that the Republic would win. The speed of the process meant that there was little opportunity for introspection or second thoughts: names had to be registered at the town hall, applications processed and medical examinations carried out. Paula remembers joining a line of hundreds of children in the open air waiting to be examined by a doctor, everyone crying. On the way to the station their big sister Paquita explained that it would be a short holiday, 'a bit of an adventure'. Then she broke the news that she herself would be staying behind in Bilbao, only the three youngest girls would be making the voyage to Southampton.

On Friday 21 May 1937 Alvaro said farewell to his tearful mother and father on the platform of Portugalete station. Alone, he walked past the barrier, beyond which only the children were allowed to go. He remembers that as he did so he turned to look at his parents, overwhelmed by the sudden realization that this might be the last glimpse he would ever have of them. 'I just looked back and see them waving and crying, then something came over me, I thought, good God, you know that sort of thing. I felt myself empty and alone.' But the train was waiting, there was no time to turn back. Alvaro joined all the other children being taken in batches of 600 to the quayside at Santurce. As the train sped out of the station it passed under a bridge thronged with parents waving handkerchiefs and calling out words of love.

On board the *Habana* it was complete bedlam. The ship was a large, but rather shabby, floating hotel. A warren of rooms and passageways bursting with people, the decks lined with rows of large wicker chairs. Everywhere swarmed disorientated and anxious children with numbered, hexagonal tags pinned to their lapels, each child carrying a little bundle of clothes. At first light the next morning, the ageing liner sailed out of Spanish waters under Royal Navy escort and across the Bay of Biscay. The ship, built for 800, was carrying five times that number. The Felipe girls knew one of the stokers on the *Habana* and he had managed to find them a sort of cabin. Nevertheless, Paula recalls the crossing was wretched:

> Conditions were great until we started. There was white bread to eat. The first time I had tasted white bread for a long time. I think I ate till I was nearly bust. Mind you, the following morning, I was sorry when the ship started to move. That Bay of Biscay could be nasty. I put my head through the port hole and all I could see was sea.[18]

For Alvaro, the torment at saying goodbye to his parents, the rough weather and his seasickness could not diminish his overwhelming excitement. For an 11-year-old boy, the *éxpediciòn a Inglaterra* was a great adventure. Paula felt scared and lonely, a 10-year-old child sailing out across the Bay of Biscay, fleeing the slaughter and chaos in her homeland. She did not return for another twenty-five years.

It was early on a rainy Sunday morning when the ship entered the waters off Southampton. She sailed passed the 'tiny fairy tale houses', so different from the tall apartment blocks of Bilbao. In the docks, the cruise liner the *Queen Mary* was moored, reducing the *Habana* to a cockleshell in comparison. Although it was still not 8 o'clock, the quayside was crammed with well-wishers. A Salvation Army band was playing as the children disembarked. Paula was fascinated by the bonnets worn by the women Salvationists. 'Do you see how they dress in this country?' she whispered to her younger sister.[19]

As they came ashore, the children were subjected to a further medical inspection and given various vaccinations. A ribbon, in one of three colours, was tied around each child's wrist. A few of the girls decided to swap their plain white ribbons for more colourful reds or blues. It was an unwise exchange. A red ribbon indicated that head lice had been found. The unlucky wearers were taken to the corporation baths to have their heads shaved.[20] From the docks, the children were ferried a few miles out of Southampton to the transit camp at North Stoneham.[21] Most went by bus, but a local taxi company provided ten cars to ferry some of the children to their new home. The route of the journey from the port to the camp was lined with bunting, flags and pictures of the royal family. The decoration had been put up to celebrate the coronation which had taken place ten days previously, but José remembers thinking 'Oh, they put it up for our benefit'. He was very impressed.

The first glimpse of the camp will always be etched on the memories of the children. What they saw were three adjacent fields in the flat Hampshire countryside covered with 500 bell tents plus larger rectangular tents for a hospital, stores and a kitchen. For many, exhilaration gave way to bewilderment. José and his brother Martín had never seen a tent before, much less slept in one. As far as the boys were concerned, tents were for Red Indians in cowboy films!

At first, everything was muddle. The final number of 4,000 refugees had been confirmed only five days previously and was double the original estimate. But, in a remarkably short time, pipes had been laid for water and gas and latrines had been dug, precarious and rudimentary structures consisting of trenches with planks. A perimeter fence of barbed wire had been made secure and was patrolled by boy scouts. Despite the assurances of the farmer that the soil was gravel and therefore very dry, it was decided to dig trenches to prevent flooding. It was a task with which many of the lads from Bilbao were all too familiar. The children were sorted into groups of between eight and ten and each group was allocated a tent. Then they were kept busy. There were elections for tent leader and competitions with prizes for the tidiest tent. Mattresses had to be stuffed with straw. When he first saw the heap of straw, one of the boys remembers being worried: 'Good God, they are not going to give us the straw to eat are they'?[22] Everywhere, there were queues. The children went constantly back and forth to the kitchen to line up for food. The queue for Horlicks was literally never ending: once you got your cup you drank it quickly and rejoined the end of the line. Food was plain but nourishing. White bread was a particular fascination and for some an obsession. There was also soup, barley or onion, noodles and corned beef. For tea, there were cakes and sandwiches. Sometimes local people brought pastries or sponge cake. A local bakery donated fifty loaves of bread to the camp each day. The children began to put on weight and regain fitness.

There were queues too for the mound of clothes and shoes that had been donated to the camp. Each child had been given a pair of waterproof boots, but the children also made forays into a great heap of second-hand clothes. Each child had left Bilbao carrying an improvised suitcase, a cardboard box tied up with string containing one change of clothes. In fact, one of the lads recalls, 'We didn't undress and soon many picked up fleas and lice'.[23] It came as a blessing that workers in the corporation wash house volunteered to work on Sundays to launder the children's clothes free of charge.

It was a British summer, that is to say there were torrential downpours that flooded tents and soaked the straw mattresses. There were also epic storms with winds that left few of the tents standing. And there were days of glorious sunshine when something like normality could prevail. Children could swarm across green fields, lines of washing could be hung out to dry; caring or curious locals could bring sweets which they passed to the children through the wire-mesh fence. Some of the children recall flashback memories of air raids. The sight of planes from a nearby airfield flying over the camp was enough to elicit uncontrollable tears. But Britain was not at war, the planes were not about to drop bombs, there was no need to run to the air-raid shelter. For these small mercies, and for the warmth and consideration with which they were treated at Stoneham, the children were hugely thankful.

The loudspeaker regulated every aspect of the children's lives. Each morning they were woken by a martial tune. 'Land of Hope and Glory' was a particular favourite. Daily instructions were given through the loudspeaker and a regime of daily exercises conducted to amplified music. It was the loudspeaker that summoned children about to be dispersed, in dribs and drabs, to other camps. It was also the loudspeaker that gave them the news, one dreadful day in June, of the fall of Bilbao. Shortly after five o'clock on Saturday 19 June 1937, the city fell to the Nationalist army. That same evening, the news was announced to the Basque children at their camp at Stoneham. The writer and political activist Yvonne Cloud witnessed the children's reactions as their world fell apart:

> A priest announced the news from a loudspeaker van. The impulse to destroy the bearer of evil news was swift. From the wailing and weeping crowd of children, swaying rhythmically in an abandonment of grief, a little knot sprang forward, rushing the van in an impotent attempt to vent their feelings of aggression.[24]

At that exact moment the children realized that their lives had changed fundamentally. None of them knew with certainty what had happened to their parents, but each child had a terrible familiarity with the way that Franco settled his scores. That night was punctuated by the sound of children weeping. The following morning they rose late and, wrote Yvonne Cloud, 'a mood of deep affliction and great sobriety hung over the camp all that day'. Little by little the sobbing died down and the daily rhythms of life were restored, but a dreadful numbness remained.

The news of 19 June was a tragedy for each individual child, but it had political implications in Britain too. Almost overnight, the mood in some quarters darkened. Sections of the British press were taken aback by the intensity with which many of the young exiles had identified with the Spanish Republic. Their grief was not just for mothers and fathers left behind, they also mourned the snuffing-out of a brave political experiment. Before the fall of Bilbao, the children were almost universally seen as the innocent victims of Guernica. Afterwards they were portrayed by some as being politically motivated: guests who had arrived under false pretences and had outstayed their welcome. Meanwhile, the children coped as best they could with events many miles away, a calamity about which they could do nothing. After a few days, some news from their homeland did start to trickle through, but for many of the children there was to be no direct contact with their parents for months or even years.

The numbers at the transit camp decreased with each passing day as children were summoned by loudspeaker to board buses that took them to more permanent homes in other parts of the country. The arrangements were at times haphazard. Seven-year-old Isabel Barrientos had sailed on the *Habana* with her two cousins. Her widowed mother had been convinced by family members to send her only child out of harm's way. While she was at the camp in North Stoneham, she developed severe toothache and was taken to the dentist for an extraction. When she returned, she found that her two cousins had vanished, having been sent to a camp in the north of England. Her loneliness was intense; she knew no one in the whole camp except a teacher from Bilbao called Doña Maria de Dios. When, a few days later Doña Maria was sent to Caerleon, Isabel went with her.[25]

Carmen Uribarri was also seven years old when she embarked upon the *Habana* with her brother Juanito. The identification label pinned to her jacket remains a clear memory for her and for many of the other refugees. Carmen was number 2879. When the children arrived in Stoneham boys and girls were sent to different parts of the camp and sister and brother became separated. So it was that Juanito ended up in Wales while Carmen was sent to the Isle of Wight.

The camp at North Stoneham closed on 18 September 1937, the weather by then having grown too chilly for children to be living under canvas. From time to time, small batches of refugees whose parents petitioned for their repatriation left for the Basque country or Catalonia, others journeyed to France or South America. But the majority of the children remained in Britain, living in homes scattered across the country. These homes, or 'colonies' as they were known, had no set pattern and, inevitably, they varied considerably in quality. The worst of them were under-funded, cramped and uncaring; the best could draw on a deep well of local support. At one end of the scale was Watermillock in Bolton, a large Victorian house in its own grounds, with playrooms, a carpentry shop and a cinema. Far less appealing were penniless orphanages like St Vincent's Home in Newcastle where, one of the teachers reported, 'there was only bread and jam for lunch'.[26]

Ministry of Labour sites, local authority properties and holiday camps were all pressed into service. The children might end up in a stately home or in a Salvation Army hostel. The Co-operative Society, the Peace Pledge Union, the Independent Labour Party and the Teachers' Association all helped sponsor colonies. The Clark family, well-known Quakers who had made their fortune in footwear, housed a group of forty-one children from anarchist families in their mansion in Street, Somerset. Three days after their arrival on the *Habana* 400 children were dispatched to the Salvation Army's centre at Clapton. It was not a success and after three months the majority of the children were relocated to other colonies

The Catholic Church took immediate responsibility for 1,200 children who came from religious backgrounds. It housed its refugees in twenty-six homes, mainly convents or orphanages. These were invariably single-sex institutions so brothers and sisters were separated. This alliance between the Church and the Basque Children's Committee was never likely to last. By September the Church had recognized Franco and the head of the Catholic hierarchy in England, Archbishop Hinsley, demanded that all the children be returned home, 'whatever the circumstances'.[27]

So it was the workings of chance, or perhaps providence, which determined that José, Martín and Alvaro would go to Brechfa, and Paula, Gerardo and Josefina to Caerleon. They could just as easily have gone to Carlisle, Colchester or any one of scores of children's colonies. One swift selection mapped out their future.

As the Basque Republic crumpled under the weight of Mola's machine a few hundred of the Basque children found refuge in Wales. There they were protected by people who from the start had been convinced of the absolute rightness of the Republican cause. They found shelter in working-class communities that were themselves cursed by atrocious poverty, but which gladly gave the little that they had. It was a kind of homecoming.

6 SHELTER FROM THE STORM

AT FIRST SIGHT Josefina thought that Cambria House was bleak and a bit overwhelming. Paula just remembers how vast the building seemed: 'I thought it was some sort of palace.' She had gone from the camp at North Stoneham to a colony in Bristol, but the experience was too traumatic: 'I couldn't take it. I felt that no bugger wanted me. Pulled from pillar to post, I had lost my confidence.' A cousin wrote asking that Paula and her two sisters be sent to Cambria House. It was a good move. Cambria House was a place of healing and settling. It provided shelter from the storm.[1]

Cambria House became home to fifty-six youngsters, six more than had been agreed on 10 July 1937. Accompanied by two interpreters and three teachers, they arrived at Newport railway station and from there were ferried by bus to Caerleon. It had been seven weeks since they had left Spain and eight days since the colony had received final approval. Through interpreters, the children were assured that they were among friends, and the local vicar, the Reverend Williams, held a brief ceremony. He told those present: 'Creeds, sects and politics should be forgotten. The only feeling should be one of sympathy for the unfortunate Spanish innocent.'[2]

Soon the old building was alive with chatter and industry. Workers provided by the council and volunteers from the university had been frantically making the former workhouse ready and it had been cleaned from top to bottom. A journalist who visited the colony the day after the children arrived saw half a dozen lads sweeping the corridors and dusting woodwork, while others worked, under supervision, in the kitchens. He reported that the children 'enter into the work with a will, and with a new pride of possession'. The speed with which the house was made ready meant that many items were in short supply and the *South Wales Argus* carried an appeal for towels, brushes, kitchen utensils, bed clothes, toys, jigsaw puzzles and picture books under the headline 'Basque Bairns want toys and towels'.[3]

It was decided that until they had learned sufficient English the children would be restricted to the grounds of Cambria House, unless accompanied by an English-speaking guide. They could, however, receive visitors. Bizarrely, on that first Sunday, the colony was visited by members of Viscount Tredegar's house party, who reportedly spoke to the children in Spanish. Evan Morgan, the second Viscount Tredegar, was a Catholic convert and a renowned eccentric. His riotous parties were notorious and his circle of friends included Aldous Huxley, Augustus John and the occultist Aleister Crowley. Quite what passed between the unconventional aristocrat and the bewildered children remains an intriguing secret.[4]

Shortly after arrival, the children were given a medical examination by Dr W. H. Reynolds and found to be in a satisfactory condition. Their emotional state was another matter. The overwhelmingly positive accounts of the children's arrival and the sincere warmth of the welcome cannot hide an undercurrent of concern. Even before the colony opened, Councillor Lovett of Caerleon had accepted that 'There were difficulties to overcome apart from the one of language.' One unsettling sentence from the accounts of that first day clarifies the nature of these difficulties: 'To prevent sorrowful reminiscences and feelings of loneliness', said an unnamed official, 'the children must be entertained and amused constantly.' The refugees were amongst friends, but no one doubted the weight of the burdens they carried.[5]

One of the most remarkable documents from Cambria House is a plea for help in shouldering those burdens: an inventory of over thirty children who were available for 'adoption'. In most cases, this would not mean full-time fostering but, rather, an appeal for a local family to offer weekend breaks, day trips or occasional holidays away from Cambria House. The ages of the children on the list range from eight to sixteen. Many are family groups of two, three, or even four siblings.

The manuscript, probably written by Cyril Cule in the summer of 1938, provides a concise description of the character of each child and, in most cases, a brief life history. Paragraph by paragraph, it exposes the heartbreaking consequences of civil war. It is a desperate, raw document that reveals the extreme vulnerability of the children in a way that seems almost intrusive to the modern reader. Even after seventy years, much of the content of those three typed sheets is upsetting, and yet the overwhelming impression is one of immense humanity.[6] Contained within a few pages is the whole history of the war in Spain. Fathers captured and held prisoner by the rebels, mothers now refugees in France or Barcelona, parents injured in air raids, whole families that have simply disappeared behind enemy lines: 'Little known of their fate.' The elder brother of three of the children was still fighting on the Madrid front. A young Basque girl remained in shock a year after she had been dug out of the rubble of her home in Rentería: it had been destroyed by a bomb. A girl of sixteen had been with her mother at Durango in March 1937 when 170 people had been killed in a church during a bombing raid. She and her mother had been talking to a man tending sheep on a hillside when the bombers came. They took cover, despite the shepherd's amusement at their fearfulness. When they came out of their shelter, they found the body of the shepherd. It was riddled with machine gun bullets.

There is scarcely a child on the list who had not been touched by personal tragedy. A 12-year-old boy was described as

> one of the nicest children at Cambria House. Slightly built, he has a calm, gentle temperament and works diligently at his lessons. His mother was injured by an air raid, but is now at Barcelona. His father, a trade unionist, has been held prisoner by the rebels for over a year. Some months ago his elder brother learnt that the father had been condemned to death and nothing has been heard from, or of him, since. This news has been kept from the lad.

And, then, there was the occasional story to keep hope alive. A brother and sister who had considered themselves orphaned after the bombing of Barcelona had their terrible anxiety ended when, weeks later, a whole batch of letters arrived from their mother.

There is a great deal of compassion in these pen portraits and the author always manages to include some detail that brings alive the child's personality. One lad is described as 'a quaint chubby little chap, with a vivid interest in everything around him'. A girl of fifteen is 'severely handicapped by deafness, though one would never suspect this when watching her intent interest in her work'. One by one, the talents of the children are celebrated: 'excels at drawing', 'clever little dancer', 'very good at knitting', 'devoted to animals', 'delights in singing', 'clever with his hands', 'knits jumpers beautifully', 'has the makings of a very fine footballer' and, when all else fails, 'filled with healthy mischief'. One of the boys, Emilio, has the word 'adopted' written across his description. He is depicted as

> a wiry little boy, about 13 years old, who is rather small for his age. He listens carefully to all that he hears and imitates perfectly. In this way, he has picked up a good working knowledge of English and can whistle like a whole aviary of birds.

There is nothing but love in these pages, not a word of criticism. Nor is there any doubt that the shattered lives of the children could be healed. The entry for a boy of nine sums up the optimism and the pathos: 'Small and dark, he is usually rather pale, for he has much to worry over . . . he is a very clever child, and if his talents are encouraged, he will probably play a useful part in the building of the new Spain.'

The staff at Cambria House were doing everything they could to lift the shadow of war from these children, but nothing can disguise the fact that many had been damaged. Exposure to mankind's capacity for extreme brutality had left its mark. Time and time again, the document makes reference to children who are still suffering from shock and who still need much care. The author carefully catalogues the cases of anxiety: 'traces of nervousness' and 'reserve tinged with fear'. Often, entries end on a hopeful note, stating that the child is gradually growing stronger and happier in Cambria House.

The warden in those early days was Gwen Jones who had previously worked in an orphanage. She was a stalwart of the Cardiff Aid Spain Committee and a member of the Young Communist League. She was not a Spanish speaker and this inability compounded other difficulties. Cyril Cule recalls that at first, discipline was extremely difficult as 'the children were in a confused state of mind and their nerves were on edge'. The warden's solution was to impose thirty-two rules. When each of these rules had been explained at great length to the assembled children, one of the older boys put up his hand and asked through a translator: 'Please ask the Señora if we are allowed to breathe.'[7]

When Maria Fernandez took over as the new warden, things began to change. To misquote Andrew Marvell slightly: 'If these are the times, then this must be the woman.' Mrs Fernandez was aged thirty-three in 1937. She had no children of her own. Her husband, Manuel, was a seafarer and often away from home. She had no formal qualifications and no education beyond elementary school. She offered her services first as translator at a time when the colony was, in her own words, 'bedlam'. It would be a pardonable exaggeration to say that she saved and sustained Cambria House. She became the heart of the colony. 'Five foot nothing and always with a broom in her hand', according to Gerardo. She ran the home her way and applied only one rule, that the children should be ambassadors for their country. 'You behaved yourself', says Paula, 'or they'd think everyone in Spain was like you.'[8]

Mrs Fernandez showed great psychological insight in the way she ran Cambria House. She said that she would have loved to have been a teacher and in another age would surely have been an outstanding educator. She did not use physical chastisement: 'I never had to punish them, ever'. Instead, she introduced a reward system with ten points being given at the start of the week and access on Friday to the tuck shop as a reward for not losing points. There had been a strict rule of not mixing with the local children but Mrs Fernandez reversed this. The first thing she did was open the doors of Cambria House. She encouraged her Basque children to play with youngsters from the town and, a few stolen apples apart, there were few problems. Knowledge of the children's Basque heritage, appeals for them to act as role models and steely determination produced results. When she arrived she was appalled to find almost all the children, even the seven-year-olds, were smoking, the children having convinced those in charge that cigarettes were an expression of Basque culture. Mrs Fernandez recalled asking one, a girl called María, what her father would do if he came round the corner and caught her smoking. 'He would give me such a smack I'd swallow the cigarette', replied the girl. 'Right', said Mrs Fernandez, 'I am your father and mother now.' Smoking was soon stamped out: 'It went, it went.'[9]

Josefina remembers that Mrs Fernandez often went about in slippers. This allowed her to emerge silently without warning. She describes one incident:

> Some boys had been showing off, visiting the old farm and taking eggs. One of the twins had his back to the door with an audience showing his ill-gotten gains. Mrs Fernandez quietly came up behind him and just looked. If she looked at you, it was enough.[10]

On another occasion some of the older boys were flicking bread around the dining room after dinner. Mrs Fernandez came in and asked them what they were doing and what their parents would say about them wasting bread. She then told them to gather all the scraps of bread and eat and eat until every leftover morsel was finished. Without water, dry bread soon lost its appeal and by the time the boys left the table, the lesson was learned. The children knew that Mrs Fernandez would keep to what she said. They knew also that she understood them and shared their dreams and fears. 'Mrs Fernandez was wonderful', said Angelita. 'If you went to her, she never refused you. She had that way about her; you could go to her for anything. Mind you, she wouldn't take no nonsense.'[11] She was fiercely proud of their achievements and did, indeed, turn them into fine ambassadors for their homeland.

The children at Caerleon produced their own monthly magazine. The *Cambria House Journal* was in part a fund-raising effort, in part a propaganda exercise, but above all the celebration of a community. Begun in November 1938, it ran for a year and in that time it covered every aspect of life in the home, from festivals and football, to the traumas of war and the pain of separation. In its pages are explanations of Basque customs, stories about pet dogs and accounts of visits to the seaside. Alongside these are descriptions of the terrifying events that drove the children into exile and their responses to the tragedy unfolding in their homeland. The *Journal* provides a fascinating record of shared experiences set against the background of momentous events. Consisting of between four and seven typewritten sheets, it was produced on an old duplicating machine. It had a print run of 4,000 and sold for 2d per copy. It was always bilingual; to begin with, almost all the articles were written in Spanish and then translated but, as the months went on, many of the children were able to write their pieces in English. Cyril Cule, the guiding hand behind the magazine, also ensured that each issue included at least a couple of sentences in Welsh. Each issue was beautifully illustrated by Eusebio Asencor, a lad from the colony, who was studying art at Newport Technical College. His exuberant cover designs of galleons, flamenco dancers or matadors often contrast with more sombre drawings on inside pages, finely drawn pictures of air raids and evacuations. Contributors, usually identified only by their initials, occasionally included staff as well as children. In the last months of the colony, family members in exile in France make a number of poignant contributions, as they chronicle the collapse of the Republic.

Throughout the *Journal*, there is appreciation for the immense kindness and generosity shown to the children: 'hospitality that has forgotten the boundaries of race and creed'. Cambria House was open every Sunday and through the doors came political allies, well-wishers and the simply curious. Local people bicycled over for the afternoon. Members of the Transport and General Workers' Union visited, as did members of the Rhondda Borough Labour Party, the Peace Pledge Union, Gloucester Co-operative Sports Club and the Women's Guild. 'Wonderful friends to us and our cause', wrote Cyril Cule.

There were also frequent invitations to visit. 'I would like to emphasize', says Josefina, 'that people welcomed us. We were invited all over the place.' Barry Girls' School played host to a group of girls, Newport Harmonic Choral Society entertained, Commercial Street Baptist Chapel in Newport threw a party for the children, followed by a film of Felix the cat and a conjuror. At the end, each child went home with the present of a yo-yo.[12] Angelita also remembered being taken to see Paul Robeson in Mountain Ash at a special concert to commemorate the thirty-three Welsh members of the International Brigade who had died in Spain. Over seven thousand people were at the gathering in the pavilion that December evening. It was a night of deep emotion. The Basque children, their hands raised in clenched-fist salutes, were given a rapturous reception. 'I have waited a long time to come down to Wales', said Robeson, 'because I know there are friends here . . . I am here because I know that these fellows fought not only for Spain but for me and the whole world. I feel it is my duty to be here.'[13] There were trips to the Cadburys factory at Bournville and gifts of broken Kit Kat from Fry's. Sometimes, the children went to stay with sympathizers for a weekend. Three times a year, after Christmas, at the end of May and again in August, the house was closed and all the children were accommodated in private homes.

At no time in its history did Cambria House go to the Basque Children's Committee for financial help. To keep the colony going cost £35 per week. £20 of the total was raised through subscriptions and £15 by fund-raising activities. The trade union guarantor group, Nonconformist chapels, clubs, even a few generous individuals, 'adopted' a child for 10s. a week. As well as guaranteeing regular income, this adoption might also involve regular letters, the occasional parcel and perhaps a weekend break. Areas were asked to form support committees and the call was answered all across south Wales: Griffithstown, Neath, Risca, Ogmore Vale, Tredegar and Abertridwr all had district committees. There were even support groups formed on the other side of Offa's Dyke; Gloucester and the Forest of Dean both raised funds and entertained parties of children. A conference of all interested parties, attended by the duchess of Atholl, president of the National Joint Committee for Spanish Relief (NJCSR), was held in Caerleon town hall on 7 January 1938.

The children themselves sang, danced, played football and sold the magazine to meet any shortfall. Above all, there was the South Wales Miners' Federation; the miners' lodges were the backbone of Cambria House. An appeal went out for the materials needed to run a school. Gifts of books and games were requested. Paper, pens, pencils, rubbers, atlases, chalk, crayons, paint-boxes, Spanish texts, picture books, bandages for first-aid classes, tools and timber for carpentry classes, clothing and material for sewing classes; all were enthusiastically given and gratefully received. Twice a year, at Christmas and in September, there were sales of work. The children spent a great deal of time making goods for these 'Spanish fairs'. The most lucrative items were models of Spanish galleons made by the boys and their teacher Mr Stephen Gibbon in the carpentry class. These galleons gained a lot of publicity for Cambria House. They were true to scale and made entirely by hand. They included a reproduction of the *Santa Maria*, the ship in which Columbus discovered America, and a fine model of an Elizabethan galleon made by Juan Antonio Hernandez.[14]

The children spent the greater part of each day at school where they were taught by two Spanish and three British teachers.[15] One of the Spanish teachers, Maria de Dios, was herself a refugee from Bilbao. The school day was longer than in some other colonies and, as far as resources allowed, no branch of their education was neglected. As well as the usual school subjects like English and arithmetic, the children had carpentry, first-aid and keep-fit lessons. They also followed events in Spain and kept up their use of Spanish. Classes, reported one observer from another colony, were well attended and well taught.[16] As one of the children wrote in the April 1939 edition of the *Cambria House Journal*, 'We did not come here to forget but rather to learn something more'. Josefina recalls that 'some of the lessons were taught by people from the university and a few of the boys, who had been out of education for some time, were not too keen on that'. She feels that, in this respect, 'education failed a lot of them and that they were happier once they got jobs'.[17] For the girls, part of each day was spent knitting woollen garments. They became expert at undoing wool donated by supporters or factory cast-offs and reusing it to knit new jumpers. What was not used in the colony was sent to Catalonia.

The children ate very well. There was porridge for breakfast and English food on Sundays, with jelly, known by the children as 'glass pudding', for dessert. Spanish food was provided by grocers in Cardiff docks and cooked by a 'gorgeous' Spanish cook,

Mrs Sancho. At tea time, the children were given a big slice of bread thickly spread with butter and, when fires were lit, they would scrape off the butter and toast the bread. But, if you left food on your plate, the remedy was a spoonful of cod liver oil.[18]

The jewel in the crown of Cambria House was the concert party. Criss-crossing south Wales and giving four or five concerts a month, it was a phenomenal success with tickets often sold out.[19] The concert party had a threefold mission: to raise funds for the colony, to build self-belief amongst the children and to spread the word about the struggle in their homeland. All the costumes worn by the choir and dancers – red shirts with a black band, black waistcoat and scarf – were made in Cambria House. To begin with, there were only girls in the company but by the spring of 1938 eight boys had joined the dance group, having been coached in the very athletic Basque dance of *Aurresku* by a student on loan from the Camberley colony. The concert programme followed a similar format wherever they performed: Spanish folk melodies and songs from the war would be interspersed with solos and recitations by local artists. There were bird imitations from Emilio and traditional folk dancing, in particular *la jota*. There was musical accompaniment from clarinets, tambourines, castanets and the *txitu* (a three-hole flute). The evening always ended with the singing of 'El Himno de Riego' (the national anthem of Republican Spain) followed by the Welsh national anthem.

In March 1939, a group of twenty-three boys and girls went on a two-week tour of south-west Wales staying with well-wishers and holding concerts in Llanelli, Swansea, Neath and Briton Ferry. The political aspect of their mission was not lost on the children. One of the children wrote about the enthusiastic reception the children had received at Briton Ferry and the obvious sympathy that was felt there for those fighting in Spain for 'the well being of all the progressive people of the world'.

The motion picture *Blockade* came to the Odeon in Newport in November 1938. Starring Henry Fonda and Madeleine Carroll, the film has now sunk into well-deserved obscurity. It told the tale of 'romance under fire'; a simple peasant during the Spanish Civil War who falls in love with a Russian woman. For a week, the children gave fifteen-minute concerts before each showing of the film. A group of six girls sang from a repertoire that included

Spanish and gypsy songs, five others danced the *jota*. Each session closed with the singing of the Welsh national anthem, 'Hen Wlad fy Nhadau'. The concerts were reportedly huge successes, with frequent demands for encores from the audience. For the girls, there was an added bonus: the chance to see the film, in which 'love versus bullets', on not one, but two occasions.[20]

Cambria House also had a mighty football team. It went by many names. Initially it was called España Libre, later it was known simply as the Basque Boys. The *South Wales Argus* called them the 'Basque Wonder Team' and by their final season they had adopted the name The Basque Unbeatables. They were, it was said, 'almost invincible'.[21] It would be difficult to overestimate the contribution that belonging to this team made to the boys' lives. Each match was of necessity played away from home and journeys, often by train, were spent singing and telling stories. By their second season, the boys were averaging one game a week, playing all over south Wales, in one month playing Aberavon, Maesteg, Merthyr Tydfil and Tredegar. The details of each victory, or narrow defeat, were written up in the *Journal*: a win, achieved against incredible odds, against Tylorstown, holding their own in Port Talbot against a team which had a great advantage over them in weight, a closely fought game in Pontypridd during which several team members distinguished themselves, but which inexplicably ended in a one–nil defeat.

After their Boxing Day game against Kitchener Road School, the boys were taken by their hosts to see Cardiff City play. Usually they went to the clubhouse where they would play ping-pong or billiards and consume huge amounts of food. 'After the game we all ate very well', wrote one of the lads. Following another game, the boys were presented with a basket of fruit, 'which pleased us very much'. At one big match, a team member almost missed the kick-off because of his fascination with the plush changing facilities, particularly the huge bath and the showers. After a successful game, he returned to the dressing room in triumph and luxuriated for half an hour under a hot shower.[22] By the time the boys returned home from their weekly escapades, it was often late in the evening and the others were already asleep. Such were the commonplace pleasures that went a little way to restore balance to the lives of boys whose childhoods had been so very chaotic.

The football team was a vital source of income for Cambria House. Programmes, which sold for 1d, contained appeals for donations of money or goods. In addition, at each game, there was a draw for the prize of a signed match ball. The games also allowed the lads to sell a good many copies of the monthly magazine at half-time, to what were often large crowds. Most importantly, the entire team had been 'adopted' by the South Wales Miners' Federation, which brought in a regular monthly income. Football also gave a substantial boost to the reputation of the Basque refugees amongst the public of south Wales. There were pre-match photographs taken of the boys with the lord mayor of Cardiff and regular match reports in the local press. An invitation came from the mayor of Newport for the boys to play at Somerton Park, the home of Newport County. The celebrated boxer Jack Petersen agreed to kick off a game and, it is said, almost scored a goal. Huge goodwill was created by the football team and this positive mood allowed the political message behind the boys' exile to reach a wide and sympathetic audience.

The culmination of the 1938–9 season was a legendary match played before thousands of spectators at Cardiff City's ground, Ninian Park. The game, on the evening of Wednesday 10 May, was against the highly regarded Moorland Road School team, league champions and winners of the Seagar Cup. The team included two schoolboy internationals and another three who played for the Cardiff youth side. It was, needless to say, 'a closely fought game'. The first half was goalless but during half-time the Moorland Road centre forward made a psychological error, saying in the hearing of the Basque team, 'we shall beat these chaps easily'. After that, the *Journal* reported, 'feelings ran high'. When Emilio Espiga scored the first goal he was carried shoulder high by his team mates. A second goal, scored by Jose Luis Acha, sealed the heroic victory. Eleven days after the game at Ninian Park, the Basque goalkeeper, Enrique Garatea, was repatriated to Spain.[23]

Reputations mattered a great deal to those who lived at Cambria House. The children were acutely aware of the malign campaign being waged against Basque refugees by the friends of Franco. In the monthly journal, they could tell their side of the story. It was a conscious attempt to counter 'the slanders of those who do not scruple to misrepresent these helpless children as murderous little wretches in order to make political capital out of their misery'. Articles by the children expressed the resentment and hurt they felt at the distorted image of their compatriots which was being peddled by the right-wing press: 'There are people who say the Basque children are criminals, that we play with knives and that we are doing harm. Is that true? No, we are not accustomed to such things.' One of the girls wrote about how pleased she was 'that the people who come on Sundays to the House do not come to speak evil of the Basque children'.[24]

In their homeland the children had witnessed sights that no child should ever see. These experiences had left their mark. Over and over again the children revisit the horrors that sent them from the land of their birth. Time and again, innocuous essays slip from relating humdrum events to describing appalling misfortune. Under the title, 'Las Vacaciones' (The Holidays), AF shares her memories of that year's Christmas festivities. Half-way through, the mood darkens as she remembers those in Spain suffering from cold, hunger and bombardments: 'What can we do to help those poor people suffering so much? All we can do is this: if we have a little money, we can send them a parcel of food, but that will not make much difference. Our pleasures came to an end and sad times came.' At the foot of the page is a brief note: 'The writer of this article has lost both her parents. She is now waiting for news of her elder sister who was a refugee in Barcelona.'[25] A straightforward article on the history of aviation by JA, entitled 'Aviones' (Aeroplanes), quickly turns into a distressing account of how 'the harmless aeroplane that brought us food from distant places now will bring us death'.

Loathing of war, 'the greatest of all catastrophes', pervades almost every issue of the *Journal*. For a long time, even after the fall of Bilbao, victory by Franco had seemed impossible. Then, the enormity of the Republic's impending defeat began to sink in. The children had to come to terms with the triumph of fascism, a triumph achieved using methods of unspeakable barbarity. At the same time, the prospect of a war which would engulf the whole of Europe grew ever closer. As their young minds grappled with the inexplicable unfairness of their defeat, the children could have been forgiven for retreating into bitterness. But they had seen too much, their experiences had made them weary of hatred. Instead, it is war itself that becomes the object of their disgust. They strove hard to articulate the depravity of what they had experienced: 'You do not realise what war means', wrote one, 'but as for me, and there are many like me, I have seen war at close quarters; I have felt it in all its crudity.'[26]

In the December 1938 issue of the *Journal*, a contributor asked the question: 'Will there come a time when men will give up their hatred and obey the sublime commandment to love one another like brothers?' Another of the children, BA, clung to the historical inevitability of mankind's one day outgrowing warfare: 'War is the greatest obstacle in the way of human progress. It destroys, annihilates and lays waste. Its action is death-dealing but sterile. Humanity marches on and upwards. Its pace is slow but sure and the goal of human perfection will be reached.'[27] A mother writing from exile, when it was known the war was lost, gave her daughter three pieces of advice: not to return to Spain; to work for a better future; and not to have feelings of hatred towards anyone.

There was solace, of a kind, to be had from retelling their stories. One unnamed girl chronicles the various stages in her exile, beginning on 11 September 1936 when she left San Sebastian as the 'traitor troops and foreigners' advanced on her city. She recalls how she fled first to Zumaya, then after a week to Marquina, and from there, in a litany of terror, on to Guernica, Durango and Baracaldo, all the time searching for a place where 'the terrible figure of Fascism had not yet established itself'. Another account describes fascist planes coming out of a magnificent summer sky to bomb Baracaldo, 'throwing out their cargo of death and destruction'. It depicts the terror as people realized that they were enemy planes, the panic as people ran for cover; the noise of anti-aircraft guns and finally the sirens signalling the all-clear.[28]

Some of the children continued to receive letters from parents who had fled Franco's advancing armies. LH received a distressing letter from his father following the fall of Barcelona. He told his son that it had been useless to go on resisting in Catalonia because of the bombardments: 'When one looked up, the first thing one saw was aeroplanes and more aeroplanes. It was horrible to see the poor mothers running and carrying children in their arms – children in need of food and clothing.'[29] C recounts the suffering of her parents as they fled into France, going from village to village, asking people if they could spend a single night under their roof. Often they slept in the open. Their letters describe seeing parcels of clothes thrown away by people who were running for their lives. At the frontier they were stopped: the price of crossing into France was 2,000 francs. They were taken to a hotel and during the night C's father had his bag stolen. The next day, the police came and threw them out into the street. 'People who passed looked at them as if they were some kind of queer animals.' Eventually, they were taken by friends to a camp near Paris. C's brother was not so fortunate. He was caught and taken to one of Franco's prison camps. There, in letters to his sister, he said: 'he is treated abominably, sleeps in the open air and the little food he gets is cold'.[30] MJA's mother worked as a matron in a Swiss-run children's home in Barcelona. In a letter to her daughter she described her experiences when trying to take the children out of Spain:

> The Swiss people wanted to take us to Switzerland but when we were at Figueras, five planes, German they were, began to bomb the town and it was all so sudden that we had to stay in a very old house, but two bombs fell so near that the house was completely destroyed and we were half dead from fear and suffocation. At last, we managed to bring the children and ourselves out of that hell of flames and ruins, and we went to the hills near the town under a rain of bombs, and when we got there some more planes came. The first five, after they dropped their load, began to machine-gun the people on the mountains, and this work of destruction went on till night.[31]

After finally finding sanctuary in France, MJA's mother wrote a letter warning her daughter against returning to Spain. But, by then, time was running out for all the refugees.

As the last days of 1938 dwindled away, there was miserable news of Nationalist forces and their Italian allies advancing on Barcelona. Many of the children in Cambria House had parents or siblings who had fled to Catalonia from the Basque country and naturally they were fearful.

That year, all that could be done to make the festive season special was done. On Christmas day, reported the *Journal*, 'there was a splendid supper for which the cook had worked enthusiastically'. That night, each child found a present next to the bed. Then, on Boxing Day, the children went to stay with friends for a week. When they returned, the traditional Spanish feast, *Fiesta de los Reyes* (Epiphany), was celebrated with a 'fine tea' attended by the mayor of Newport. Father Christmas gave out toys from beneath a Christmas tree. There were games too; the favourite involved being blindfolded and stamping on balloons. 'After this enjoyable evening', wrote one young contributor, 'the bell rang and we all went to bed hoping to spend the whole year with the same happiness and enjoyment'.[32]

It is clear that there was something out of the ordinary about Cambria House. Each day had certainty and steadiness. There was a gentle routine that was balm to children still bruised from dreadful experiences. MZ wrote about the comforting rhythm of a typical day:

> If you come one day to visit Cambria House, you will see us very happy. If you come in the morning you will see Mrs Sancho holding a bell and making it ring; then we get up and we make the beds and after we get ready to eat our breakfast and clean the house; after Mrs Sancho rings the bell again we go to school.[33]

It is the simple pleasures and innocent mischief that the children recall: improvising games of pelota against the wall, learning to play cricket indoors and hitting a chandelier, scrumping apples and pears, walking in the fields and swimming in the lido. After returning to Cambria House following a summer holiday, Christobal wrote: 'It was fine to come back to something that exists in so few places in this troubled world – the spirit of complete equality, comradeship and mutual confidence between the children, warden and staff.' A recent arrival from another colony said: 'I have been with my comrades in several different places and I notice the difference between them and this one.'[34] As Paula says: 'Caerleon was a happy home; I don't remember any badness there.'

7 DASTARDLY YARNS

ON THE BAR of the Forest Arms Hotel in Brechfa, black and sleek, was a stuffed raven. In life, the bird had been the landlord's pet, 'the scourge and delight' of the village. He had been given the name Bob and many stories were told about his escapades flying across the wooded hills of Cwm Cothi. Such was the bird's fame that in 1933 it had featured in a series of a short essays by Gareth Jones, a journalist with a worldwide reputation. Jones tells how, one afternoon in 1933, he descended from the slopes of Pencrugmelyn into the village to 'stand in awe before the bird of Brechfa' and to chat with the landlord, Joe Sivell.[1]

According to Gareth Jones, Sivell was a 'rare host', always ready with a story from his younger days when he had worked as a groom and coachman. Joe and his four sons, Doe, Bertie, Dudley and Kim, ran the inn and organized fishing trips. The river Cothi was famous across Britain for its fishing. There were fisherman's tales of landing 42 lb salmon and visiting anglers were treated like lords. In the 1930s, the Forest Arms became the hotel of choice for many well-heeled visitors. On one occasion, a local recalls that there were no fewer than six Rolls Royce cars parked outside the hotel. The owner of the Lewis group of stores, Rex Cohen, who was a regular guest, presented the inn with a full-sized billiard table. Clough Williams Ellis, the architect, stayed at the hotel, as did George Bernard Shaw. The world-famous playwright detested angling but he and his wife Charlotte sought solitude by walking in the gentle, wooded hills around Brechfa. 'No one ought to be in government in this land', wrote Shaw, 'who does not spend three months of the year in such country as this.'[2] Another guest at the Forest Arms was the celebrated rugby player Prince Alexander Obolensky. To the delight of the local boys, the 'scorer of the greatest try of all time' drove up to the inn in a white Lanchester. It is an event which is talked about to this day.

The arrival of a band of adolescent exiles into this otherworldly and rather lucrative idyll caused quite a stir. Roy James, now eighty-four years old, has lived all his life in the village of Abergolech just outside Brechfa. He well remembers the arrival of the Basque boys in his corner of Carmarthenshire. As a young lad of thirteen, Roy and a group of his pals cycled the mile and a half to Cynarth camp. There, peering through a newly cut gap in the hedge, they saw for themselves the exotic newcomers. They were, he recalls, 'a wild eyed bunch, brown as berries and wearing short raggedy trousers'.[3]

No one would argue that Cynarth Training Camp at Abergolech, 2 miles south of the village, was an ideal location to house refugees. Situated near the river, it was in the lee of Llanmynydd, a wooded hill which a century before had been a haunt of the Rebecca Rioters. The location was intended as a stopgap measure while negotiations took place for a more hospitable site: Bronwydd Mansion or Felinfoel House in Llanelli were both under consideration. In the meantime, the Ministry of Labour had consented to its disused training centre being used as a colony, provided the Basque Children's Committee assumed complete financial responsibility. So it was that on 16 July 1937, seventy-two boys, aged between eight and fifteen, found themselves deposited in the middle of the Carmarthenshire countryside.[4]

The reaction of many of the boys to their new home was one of shock. One of the refugees reportedly told a local resident that he and his friends would prefer to go back to Spain and be shelled than remain in the camp. Most had been uprooted from the industrialized city of Bilbao. They had lived in apartment blocks in closely knit working-class districts. Now they had been set down in a cold and inhospitable training camp in the parish of Brechfa, beautiful but remote and rustic. Moreover, they had no idea when they would be going home. Bilbao had fallen to Franco on 19 June so the original promise of a return home within three months became unthinkable. The pages of the local newspapers reflect the highly charged atmosphere of those months. The general approach was to suspend judgement on the wisdom of accepting refugees, although there were a few warning signs in an account published in the *Welshman* newspaper at the time of the boys' arrival in Brechfa:

> Reports have appeared in the press lately of indiscipline on the part of the boys at certain of the camps and it is understood that the party at Brechfa includes some youths whose behaviour has not been of the best. On behalf of these lads it is pointed out that many of them have been entirely undisciplined for over a year since the trouble started in Spain, but under the supervision of their teachers there is every prospect of an improvement in their behaviour.[5]

The welcome from local politicians was also ambivalent. Just prior to the opening of the Brechfa camp, the Public Assistance Committee of Carmarthenshire County Council had debated a request by the Basque Children's Committee to accommodate twenty to thirty children in Llanelli. One councillor strongly opposed the idea, arguing that the children were a 'dangerous lot', while another described them as a 'menace'. The prevailing view, expressed by one alderman, was that 'we have to look after our own children first; there is not sufficient accommodation to warrant being generous'. The committee duly rejected the request.[6]

The camp had only four staff. It was in the charge of Mr F. P. Ashe of the Ministry of Labour, who was assisted by a young Spanish-American man, Enrico Egurale, and two college graduates. Amongst the boys in their care were many who had experienced almost daily bombardments. Others had been conscripted for labour in the trenches around Bilbao, at a time when all possible labour was being requisitioned. There was next to no supervision at the camp, no structure to the day and no schooling. José Armolea remembers arriving at Brechfa. He was eleven years old.

> We got off the coach and we realized we were on our own with only one man in charge of about fifty boys and nobody to greet us. The camp was a collection of Nissan huts that had been used by sick and unemployed miners. It was a beautiful spot, out in the wild and on a slight incline. There was an urn in the middle of the camp full of cocoa and lots of corned beef sandwiches that we ate for days afterwards. We had to fill our mattresses with straw, which we then put over three slats of wood to sleep on. No sheets. In the morning, there was the same cocoa and sandwiches and that was our meal for I don't know how many days. The Brechfa people were snooty and well off. They didn't want us there from day one. Mind you I'm not saying that we were angels. We arrived at a camp with all that freedom, a kilometre or so from the nearest village with only one person looking after us. What is going on? We were in a situation where we had no supervision. We could do anything we wanted. No schooling, no proper meals. After a while kids started venturing out. How do you expect kids to behave?[7]

The trouble started on the Thursday evening, exactly a week after the boys had arrived. A visitor from Yorkshire staying at the Forest Arms Hotel, returned from a fishing trip on the river Cothi to find three or four lads from the camp gathered round, or perhaps even sitting in, his motor car which was parked in a field. The car window had allegedly been damaged and the owner was understandably angry. According to press reports, he went to the camp to complain to the supervisor and the boys resented this. The surviving *niños* (children) remember it a little differently. They recall the boys retreating to the camp following a shouting match with the car owner, the landlord and his son which turned violent. It is likely that one of the Basque boys was kicked quite badly. José recalls:

> I remember it very, very well. Some of the older lads returned later that night to settle the score. Nobody was going to push them around. I was told to stay in the

camp. My brother was in the older group and I was getting my orders from him.

Twenty or more marched back to the town having first raided the stores for table knives. 'It might not have been all of us but most of us went to the village and smashed the windows', admits Alvaro. They threw stones at the Forest Arms and shattered practically every pane. The landlord, Mr Sivell, told reporters:

> One fellow came to the door brandishing a dagger three feet long, with which he threatened me. Several of my guests including two army captains helped me to keep the Basques away from the doors as they tried to come in. The refugees then retired to the roadway and a brick came hurling through the window and just missed me. Stones came in through nearly every window. We gathered a wheelbarrow of stones from various rooms this morning.[8]

When the owner of the neighbouring Tŷ Mawr cottage reprimanded one of the lads they stoned his house too. His wife was too terrified to remain in the house. The *Carmarthen Journal* reported that the people of the district went about in fear and trepidation. One of them pleaded: 'For heaven's sake take them away from here. We are afraid to sleep in our beds at night.'[9]

There is an alternative version of events, put forward by Mr C. Lloyd Humphreys, the secretary of the Spanish Children's Fund, who, accompanied by a Spanish interpreter, visited the camp three days later. He alleges that a 14-year-old Basque boy was looking after the official camp car when a person came out of the inn, pulled him to the ground, beat and kicked him. The other boys, outraged by this assault, marched to the village to protest. When they got to the public house they were, he alleges, confronted by two men armed with double-barrelled shotguns. 'The boys naturally got excited and shouted, "they are going to shoot, get stones", they gathered stones and threw them. Some windows were broken.'[10] Police were called and about a dozen officers from Carmarthen and Llandeilo arrived on motorcycles. By then, most of the boys had gone back to the camp, but a few continued to roam the countryside.

The next day, the boys resumed their disorderly conduct. The local papers breathlessly reported each outrage. Barrels of tar left on the roadside by council workmen had been moved to block the road. A number of the lads had apparently forced a chest in the camp cookhouse and armed themselves with steel table knives, 'some of which had been sharpened to dagger point'. Other knives were later found hidden under bedding. Police Constable David Evans of Pencader had a knife thrown at his car, 'missing the officer's head by inches'. Mr Lewis Lewis of Fronhaul, the local blacksmith, reported that a grindstone which was in front of his smithy had to be removed hastily, because it was feared that if the boys got hold of it they would cause some destruction. A young lady was reportedly thrown off her bicycle by the Basque boys, and the machine taken from her.[11]

One resident said that the boys were absolutely out of control. 'It was a proper riot here last night', he said. 'There are about fifteen ringleaders among the boys. My own car was struck with a stone. One of the supervisors came up to apologise to me and advised me to drive off, otherwise I should have every window broken.'[12]

What followed was officially described as a 'short and sharp skirmish', but Alvaro Velasco uses a more expressive phrase. 'The police', he says, 'gave us a pasting.' José Ármolea remembers more than twenty boys being stopped on the way to Brechfa by a coach-load of police, truncheons drawn. The boys scattered, some crossing the river fully clothed in an effort to escape. The boys were generally better runners than the police, but anyone caught was hit either with fists or truncheons. The wrongdoers were pursued back to the camp where the police banged on the metal roof of the huts, while the terrified younger boys inside hid under their beds.[13] Three of the boys were then taken to Newcastle Emlyn police station where they were charged with taking away a motor car without the owner's consent. They were remanded in custody for a week pending instructions from the Home Office. Some of the boys later complained about the treatment they had received, but allegations about assaults or about the conduct of the police were dismissed as a distraction. The boys had got what they deserved.

Blame for the disturbances was fixed squarely on a group of about fifteen boys who were variously described as intractable, troublesome or, simply, 'bad'. It was claimed that these 'desperadoes' had been 'uncontrollable in other places', although there is no direct evidence for this. 'These were not', insists José Armoleo, 'a group of hard-nuts: they were ordinary kids.' Indeed, the capacity to separate potential troublemakers from more cooperative children almost certainly exaggerates the degree of organization that had existed at Southampton. The camp supervisor Mr Ashe stated that he was sorry such prominence had been given to the misdemeanours of a few and that only fifteen of the seventy-two had given cause for complaint.[14]

The Basque Children's Committee moved quickly to try to limit the damage from the Brechfa incident. That Saturday, David Rhys Grenfell, the Labour MP for the Gower, visited the camp where he found the boys 'in a highly nervous state, liable to become excited by suggestions of the older boys'. In a public statement on 5 August, Grenfell chose his words with great care: 'we think the boys were provoked to a certain extent and a little roughness was possibly used in one or two cases in quelling the unrest'. Whatever the truth of the provocation, there is no disputing that matters had got out of hand. By the following Monday, arrangements were in place for the fifteen most troublesome boys to be removed from the camp. The next day, Mr Wilfred Roberts MP, on behalf of the National Joint Committee for Spanish Relief, announced that the boys would be sent back to their home areas of Spain. He described them as suffering from shell shock and nervous breakdown and gave their ages as between thirteen and seventeen.[15]

The letter pages of the Carmarthenshire papers spluttered with fury. Mr de Waal Davies, a visitor to the Old Country from Cape Town, related how he had motored over to Brechfa to see for himself what type of boys they were. He found them 'an ill-mannered and importunate lot'. Captain George Pryse-Saunders of Kidwelly wrote to denounce the behaviour of the 'rowdies' and demand that they be shipped back to fight for whichever side they wish to support in their own country. 'Surely', he added, 'we already have in our own country sufficient unemployed and people who suffer from poverty without adding to the numbers.' The anonymous 'Observer' wrote with apparent reasonableness. The boys should not be blamed, he said, they should be pitied.

They had seen gruesome slaughter and their young minds had been contaminated. 'Most of them are in a highly nervous state, perhaps bordering on insanity.' Fortunately, he had a solution: segregate the 'big bad boys' in a confined area where their chances of damaging private property would be nil.[16]

At the quarterly meeting of Carmarthenshire County Council held on the Tuesday after the disturbances, councillors and aldermen lined up to express their indignation. Alderman W. D. Davies led the attack. He felt that there must have been some gross negligence on the part of someone. The children were not under proper control and supervision. As a result of the riots, parents were afraid to send their children to school. Some people were trying to whitewash the position, he alleged; such people should speak to the people of Brechfa or go to the village to see for themselves the results of the actions of the refugees. Alderman Watkins added that he had been told that if the refugees had had their way they would have burned down the thatched cottage which they attacked in the village. Councillor Edgar Lewis suggested the setting up of a committee of inquiry and the clerk was instructed to issue an ultimatum to those responsible for sending the Basque boys to Brechfa: either put them under control or remove them. The overwhelming feeling of the meeting as reported in the local press was that those living in peaceful, quiet countryside were entitled to protection.[17]

Then the fever passed. Now, for every question asking, 'why place such children in the peaceful Welsh countryside?', there was an answer: 'it's all very well to send them away from Brechfa, but where will they go?

The owner of Pantycerrig farm on which the camp was situated said that he had received no complaints from his tenant regarding the boys' behaviour and that no damage had been done to his farm at all. The majority of refugees were 'decent little kids'. Another resident said that 'there was not one to whom you could take a dislike'. Councillor J. Ll. Evans, the Llanelli organizer of the Basque Refugee Committee, made an appeal for understanding and sympathy: 'Some of these children had seen terrible things at a very impressionable age. They have seen their parents machine gunned and their homes blown to smithereens. We would be ill-advised to fan the flames of criticism against the Basque children.'

Lord Davies, who inaugurated the Welsh refugee fund, asked that the public keep matters in proportion. 'Too much stress should not be laid on isolated cases of young people acting in this fashion', he said. 'Boys will be boys and the whole scheme of relief afforded to these unfortunate children should not be condemned because of a few instances of insubordination on the part of one or two of them.'[18] Earlier, even the *Western Mail* had appealed for tolerance. It emphasized the shocking condition of many of the children: 'Outwardly they were happy and contented, but thin bodies and sunken cheeks spoke eloquently of their suffering.'[19] The weeks passed and the mood softened.

After 'the incident', the boys' lives changed for the better. Almost at once, like the Seventh Cavalry riding to the rescue, busloads of visitors arrived at the camp from nearby Carmarthen. The townsfolk came to express fellow feeling with the children and through them with the people of Spain. In countless gestures of quiet humanity, they dismantled the underlying mood of hostility and restored relationships with the evacuees. The fracas outside the Forest Arms Hotel counts for very little in José's memory when set against such kindness and solidarity.

> This is the beauty of it. From a situation when nobody cared, we went to one where every child had a foster family. They were ever so good. After our troubles they came in buses – ordinary working people, with presents. They came every Sunday afternoon after the troubles. Each one of us had a family that came to visit. These people came when they heard of the difficulties we were in. They didn't know we were there before.[20]

It was a glorious, sun-baked summer. There had been no rain at all for eighteen consecutive days and temperatures were higher than 70° Fahrenheit. In mid-August, some rain finally did arrive but not enough to spoil holiday prospects. 'The shower', the Air Ministry reported lyrically, 'was little heavier than a fall of dew'. The boys filled their days by swimming in the river. Exasperated local anglers found the flow of the Cothi altered by dams made of pebbles. Visitors from town would drop pennies into the pools formed by these dams; the boys dived to retrieve the coins. The long summer gave the boys a chance to perfect their football skills in a clearing in the camp. The boys' soccer team, the Red Lions, played a series of matches against local sides, the highlight being a game against the Welsh-Spaniards at Abercraf. Football kit for the team was provided by the local Labour MP Jim Griffiths. Carmarthen cycle club arranged trips to nearby beaches and the town cinema donated free tickets. Each boy had a family who would come to visit him by bus on a Sunday, often with a small present. One Sunday Alvaro remembers being brought some bananas. José was given a suitcase in which to keep his possessions, an act of kindness by his 'Carmarthen family' that he remembers to this day.[21] Over seventy years later, Alvaro's gratitude to the ordinary folk of Carmarthen also remains vivid and heartfelt:

> Repeating and repeating, because I can never say it too often, the people of Carmarthen took us to their hearts. The Unions and the Salvation Army both were very good to us. In Mill Street and Cambrian Place the poorest of people would give us their last penny. We, the children, would be taken for tea every Tuesday and Sunday. They were very, very good to us. I didn't want to go back.[22]

By now, there were eleven workers at the camp, at least two of them from the Spanish community at Abercraf.[23] Their nominal wages paid by the National Joint Committee. In addition to these helpers, there was a plethora of women from Carmarthen who had been given the job of helping out with the provision of food and clothing. The children, according to one of these volunteers, were 'delightful, friendly and scrupulously clean'.[24]

The Basque Children's Committee had promised immediately after the troubles that every effort would be made to transfer the children at Brechfa to another place, 'if possible a town where they will feel more at home'. In any case the cold, damaged camp at Abergolech was not a suitable place to spend winter. On 16 September, the children were moved to Bronwydd, which Alvaro remembers as an empty, crow-ridden mansion near Newcastle Emlyn. A Llanelli businessman, Ben Evans, had agreed terms for the disused house, the former home of Sir Marteine Lloyd, to be used as a safe haven for the Brechfa boys. The house, an elaborate Victorian castle, straight out of a Hans Christian Andersen fantasy, came complete with a baronial hall, round tower and bell turret.[25] The boys, Alvaro and José amongst them, stayed in this Gothic fantasy until 29 October 1937 and were then dispersed to a colony near Margate. In time, and with varying degrees of reluctance, the majority were returned to Spain.

Generosity for the dispossessed and meanness of spirit towards outsiders were in contention throughout that summer. The arrival of the refugees in May had been accompanied by an outpouring of fellow feeling. It took a skirmish in the Welsh countryside to reawaken the hostility felt by some for the whole project. In normal times the unruly behaviour of a few boys would not have seemed so very terrible, but the political mood that summer was far from normal. The war in Spain polarized British public opinion and in that fevered atmosphere the incident in Carmarthenshire was seized upon by those who had never wanted the refugees in this country in the first place. The clamour to 'send them all home' became louder and suddenly seemed more legitimate. Brechfa was significant because it offered an opportunity to portray the Basque refugees as political, ungrateful and violent.

The process of demonizing the refugees had begun a month earlier with the panic-stricken reaction of some the children to the fall of Bilbao. Three hundred children broke out of the camp that evening in 'wild and grief-stricken purposelessness'.[26] Such scenes were a propaganda gift to those with axes to grind. From that point onwards the right-wing press did what it could to chip away at the images that had made the Basque children objects of public sympathy. The refugees were branded as unstable and ungrateful. In a quite unscrupulous campaign, the image of decent, moderate and vulnerable children became distorted. As the American historian Dorothy Legarreta observed, 'from that moment they had a handle on destroying sympathy'. Similar tactics were used to blacken the image of refugees in France and Mexico.[27]

The troubles at Brechfa had greater resonance because they were linked in the public imagination with another, more trivial incident at Harwood Dale near Scarborough. The site there was described by one observer as little better than a penal colony.[28] Like Brechfa, it was a former Ministry of Labour camp, and it housed two hundred of the 'most rebellious boys'. The welcome these boys received when they arrived on 7 July was distinctly tepid. Scarborough Corporation had made it quite clear that no children would be allowed into the town itself until the tourist season was over. Things did not go well. After complaints from the boys about the food, there was a riot and the camp cook was chased until he took refuge in a nearby farmhouse. It took four police constables and an inspector to restore order and by then windows had been broken and damage done to the camp.

Parliament rose for the summer recess that week, but three MPs managed to put in written questions about the lawless behaviour of the Basque children. The Conservative MP, Sir Thomas Moore, asked the home secretary, 'In view of the repeated attacks made on British citizens by refugee Basque children, will he consider making arrangements for an early return to their own country?' Another backbencher, Vice-Admiral Taylor, asked, 'whether in view of the riotous conduct of the Basque refugee children, he proposes to take action to repatriate them?' It was left to the local Labour MP, Daniel Hopkin, to suggest that the whole disturbance could have been avoided with proper supervision. The Home Office minister, Mr G. Lloyd, made a calming statement in reply:

> There have been one or two regrettable outbreaks of disorderly behaviour amongst the Basques, but my information is that these had been entirely local in character and have been caused by a few of the older boys. It has been decided to repatriate the boys responsible for the disturbances, about 24 in number, and it is expected they would leave before the end of the week.[29]

Unsurprisingly, there were lurid headlines in right-wing newspapers. The headline for the *Sunday Dispatch* article was 'Night of terror by hooligans who must go'. A strident editorial in the *Daily Mail* called for the 'Basque terrors to be transferred', while another newspaper used a contrived witticism to make its point with the caption, 'Put all these Basques in one exit'.[30] Even American newspapers reported the disturbance. It is a fair bet that the village of Brechfa has not featured often on the pages of the *New York Times*. However, on 24 July 1937, the prestigious daily carried the story of the 'rioting' and, the following day, provided further vivid detail of 'Basque refugee boys armed with table knives and sticks [who] fought policemen in the village of Brechfa, Wales'. On Friday 30 July, a rather blurred photograph appeared in several of the Fleet Street morning papers. It showed a group of eight Basque refugee boys about to board an evening train from Waterloo station. It was reported that they were being escorted back to Spain by Mr Edward Lawrence, a teacher of languages. The boys are smiling broadly, their hands raised in the clenched-fist communist salute.

The campaign to portray the Basque children as 'red terrorists' undoubtedly had an impact on public opinion. After Brechfa, the feeling grew that something had gone wrong. Brechfa was not the start of this process, rather, it was the reaction to the fall of Bilbao. Nor was it the only riot, there had been Scarborough. But events in Bilbao occurred too soon after the initial enthusiasm and the incident at Scarborough was not sufficiently vivid. One measure of the success of the process of demonization is that in the months that followed, a decreasing amount was given in donations to the Basque Children's Committee. An article in the committee's bulletin of March 1938 acknowledged this shift in public perception. Under the headline 'Intrigues against the children – a wicked campaign', it stated that 'it must be clearly understood that the campaigns to which the children have been subjected have very seriously affected our funds'.

The change in public mood can also be seen in protests from communities opposed to the housing of Basque refugees in their area. Villagers in Elford, Staffordshire, expressed their hostility to a proposal to house sixty children at Elford Hall. They were concerned, they said, for the peace of their village and were apprehensive about possible damage to the 'almost priceless wonders of the parish church'. The decision was clearly influenced by events in Brechfa less than a fortnight earlier. The chairman of the parish council said that, from what they had read, 'the refugee children had generally ran amok and upset all the districts where they had been placed'.[31] The day before, the townsfolk of Castleton in the Peak District had expressed similar fears about a proposal to send twenty-five Basque children to the nearby camp at Hollowford.

Above all, shifting attitudes can be seen in the defensive tone of communications from the Basque Children's Committee and in articles in support of the refugees that appeared in various periodicals. In August, the committee wrote to each of its supporters to denounce the 'alarmist, mischievous and untrue paragraphs in the national and local press'. It was concerned that these reports might 'endanger the universal goodwill and generosity with which the children have been welcomed to this country'. It then attempted to fend off criticism of the refugees, stressing that the children 'have naturally excitable nervous systems' and that the Ministry of Labour camps 'may have given the boys the impression that they were in a concentration camp'. It concluded by attempting to put matters into context: 'accounts of damage in the press have been greatly exaggerated. A few pounds will cover the claims made by residents in the neighbourhood of these two camps. Far greater damage has been done by public schoolboys and university students, frequently without press comment.' The document had been designed as a damage limitation exercise; instead, it fed public anxiety and contributed to a sense of grievance.[32]

A contributor to the *New Statesman* magazine expressed incredulity and revulsion at the hostile manner in which the children's reaction to the fall of Bilbao had been portrayed. He also said that he believed that reports of boys 'terrorising the countryside' at Brechfa were entirely distorted. What would happen, he wondered, if 4,000 children were taken from Brighton to Madrid at a time of civil war and then told that their home town had fallen to the enemy and that there was no word of their parents? 'I am quite sure that the same "mass hysteria" and "rioting" would occur even in the absence of a Spanish temperament.'[33] In *John Bull* magazine, an article entitled 'The stark truth' described the refugees as 'invalids' and said that, 'though they have been here nearly three months, their eyes are still wide with terror'. It concluded that the trouble at Brechfa had been the result of a failure of communication caused by the refusal of the Home Office to allow adult Spanish speakers into Britain to act as interpreters.

> Actually the total damage caused at Brechfa and another disturbance at Scarborough was less than £10. The total number of boys sent in disgrace to France is seventeen

> . . . But seventeen out of 4,000 does not seem to us a high proportion, nor does the fact that there has been trouble in only three out of seventy camps.[34]

The disturbances in Brechfa sent shock waves through many communities that had previously been rock solid in their support for the Basque refugees. Llanelli was 24 miles from Brechfa and, by any standards, the efforts of the people of the town on behalf of the exiled children had been extraordinary. Built on tin smelting and heavy industry, 'Tinopolis' remained strongly Welsh speaking and was on the cusp of rural and industrial Wales. It was a town with a sturdy reputation for extra-parliamentary protest. In 1911, during a rail strike, two men had been shot by troops, properties were blown up and four men killed in an explosion. The same year, the town's schoolchildren marched through the streets in their own 'schoolboys' strike' in protest against the caning of a pupil. Given its radical past, it is not surprising that solidarity with the Spanish Republic was strong in the town, a mood intensified in the summer of 1936 when a Llanelli man, William Morris, was killed while fighting for the International Brigade in Brunete.

There was extensive support for the establishment of a home for Basque children in the Llanelli area. On 24 June, ninety delegates had met to launch a fund-raising appeal.

The initial list of donors shows sizeable financial contributions from the Band of Hope and the YMCA, as well as more predictable groups like trade unions and foundry workers. Within a month, the town's Spanish Children Fund had raised £68.[35] The vigour of those first weeks was given shape in a series of town meetings. By the time the children arrived in Wales, the townsfolk had pledged to raise enough money to provide for twenty Basque refugees. This took a phenomenal amount of coordination and the active involvement of trades unions, chapels and schools. The powerhouse behind this huge organizational effort was Mr C. Lloyd Humphreys, a master at the town's county school.

A levy of 1d per week for each working member was agreed by over a thousand trade unionists; deductions were made either to union collectors or direct from the pay packet by management. Ten local churches held monthly collections and various clubs and societies also contributed regular amounts. Committee members addressed trade union branches and approached church leaders, in an effort to raise cash as well as consciousness.[36] In early July, a rally for Peace in Europe was held in the market hall; addressed by the Labour leader Clement Attlee and the local MP Jim Griffiths, it concluded with a collection for the Basque children. In this way, a steady income was built up and by March 1938 donations to the Basque children's committee had passed the £500 mark.

Yet, even in such a closely knit and progressive community, active sympathy for the Basque refugees was not universal. Events in Brechfa meant that misgivings about the entire project no longer had to be concealed. At a bad-tempered council meeting held at the end of July, town councillors voted by 11 to 7 votes not to affiliate to the Spanish Children's Fund. A 'lively scene' ensued when the mayor of the town, Mr J. H. Williams JP, gave his reasons for refusing to join the local committee: 'While not lacking in sympathy with suffering children in Spain,' he said, 'I submit there is equal need in our own town and district. Sympathy, charity and love should begin at home.'[37]

Over and over again, the spectre of Brechfa was raised to justify opposition to the whole refugee project. Allegations were made that some councillors were trying to excuse the boys' behaviour by exaggerating the poor state of the camp. The two communist councillors were accused of spreading lies about conditions in Brechfa. Such 'dastardly yarns' were too much for Alderman W. E. Davies. He had been to the Brechfa camp dozens of times: 'My dear boy, I was there last Tuesday.' In his opinion, 'there was not a cleaner or finer placed camp'. Another councillor suggested that criticism of the council for failure to help the refugees would be better directed at Hitler and Mussolini. In the uproar that followed the mayor threatened to suspend the meeting. Councillor Bryn Thomas spoke for those who still wanted to open a home for the refugees in the town:

> It is felt that in getting the children to Llanelli under the care of women much good would be done. Surely, we are as humane as Swansea. At present, these children are like rabbits in the wilderness of the North Pole. I should be sorry to see dogs where these children are. It is horrible. I found the little chaps pleasant and well behaved

> but poorly clad and shod. The food they receive is heart-breaking. I have seen suffering in Llanelli but you would have to go a long way to see conditions like those at Brechfa camp. I am not exaggerating.[38]

But the damage was done. The fund organizers reported that there had been a significant change in attitude: 'People who were well disposed at first are now hostile.' There was a feeling among some in the town that the committee was trying to 'import a gang of young murderers'. The attempt to find a suitable home in Llanelli for twenty refugees was stillborn. Eleven potential houses had been considered, all but one refused. The remaining house was prohibitively expensive. The treasurer, John James, said that he was 'sick and tired'.[39] Try as they might it proved difficult to shake off the controversy.

However, in Llanelli, as elsewhere in Wales the harm done by the disturbances in Brechfa did not last. Fellow feeling towards the children reasserted itself. In September, the committee was able to report that they had obtained the lease on a 'beautiful mansion set in its own grounds'. The lease of Bronwydd rescued the boys from Brechfa and from an increasingly cold and uncomfortable camp. It also redeemed Llanelli's reputation as the town in Wales that contributed most to the cause of the Basque exiles.

The brawl in Brechfa was a relatively trivial event. It gained significance when it became a crucial part of a campaign that had been gaining momentum since the fall of Bilbao. The disturbance allowed Franco's apologists in the Church, press and Parliament to seize back the initiative by claiming that the children had a communist background and linking this with violent behaviour. In this way, an attempt was made to dismantle any sense of solidarity with the young refugees.

8 A TIDAL WAVE OF GIVING

ANTONIA LAPERA was born in Bilbao in 1912. The eldest of three children, she was brought up on Calle Zavala, a winding road that led to the outskirts of the city and upwards onto a mountain path. On saints' days, young girls would dance the *jota* along this road, following the fife and drum man all the way to the beauty spot of San Roque. One of these dancing girls was Antonia's sister, Lola. The youngest of the three siblings, she was always getting into trouble and fighting with other youngsters in the neighbourhood. The two girls shared a second-floor flat with their brother Pedro, their mother Manuela and two aunts. From time to time, the family kept a goat there and possibly – memories clash on this point – a chicken. Manuela kept the family together by taking in washing and sewing. Her husband, Vicente, had died in America sometime in the late 1920s or early 1930s. He had been a stoker in the merchant navy, seeing his family only on those rare occasions when his ship was in port. When they left school, the girls helped support the family by finding work, Antonia as a shorthand typist and her sister as a butcher's assistant.

The Lapera family were aware of their working-class roots and supported the Republic. Manuela was a socialist, attending impromptu meetings, raising her hand in a clenched-fist salute. At the same time, her eldest daughter embraced Catholicism, going on trips to the countryside organized by the church and even at one point considering a vocation as a nun. When the Civil War took hold, she felt, she said, like a piggy in the middle, not fully accepted by either side. As nationalist forces advanced on Bilbao, the decision was taken to evacuate as many Basque children as possible. Manuela took both her daughters to the committees that were formed by the political parties to register children and carers. Lola was allocated a place on the *Habana* but her elder sister, 'always in church Antonia', was refused.

Antonia was not daunted for long by this setback. A neighbour had a boyfriend who worked as a mechanic on a coal boat and, when the *Polliak* sailed out of Bilbao, Antonia was among several hundred refugees on board. On disembarkation at La Rochelle, everyone was deloused and taken on a second voyage by trawler to Bordeaux where they collected their luggage. The refugees were then split up into small groups of twenty and dispersed to surrounding villages. Antonia found herself housed in an old people's home run by nuns. The beds were crawling with bugs but she was too exhausted, physically and emotionally, to care. One morning, she remembers waking up to find that uninvited and unnoticed, an old man had slipped into her bed during the night.

It was the kindness of two strangers that rescued Antonia. She was befriended by a young couple who gave her enough money to get to Le Havre and from there on to Southampton, the English port where the *Habana* had docked a month earlier. At North Stoneham camp she found that her sister had already departed and was working as a kitchen helper in a colony outside Swansea but, having come so far, there would be no faltering on the last lap. It was agreed that Antonia would also be found a place in Wales and the authorities even arranged a lift in the car of a visiting committee member. So it was that the two sisters were finally restored to one another, Antonia arriving in style at Sketty Park House, an enormous residence set in a beautiful park with echoes of the big estates outside Bilbao. Lola welcomed her sister's unexpected arrival with a mixture of astonishment and joy. It was a happy reunion, welcomed by everyone, or almost everyone, in Sketty Park.[1]

Lola and the children had already been in Swansea for a week. They had arrived by train on 30 June 1937, a day earlier than had been expected. There had been a mad panic to sort out buses to take them from the railway station. Identified by labels around their neck, the children had first to be photographed and registered. Then they emerged into the square in front of the station to find it thronged with people. As they caught sight of the children, the people in the crowd began to clap fiercely. The youngsters were surrounded by well-wishers and showered with sweets and small gifts as they clambered onto the two waiting buses. The warmth of the welcome from ordinary working people made an unforgettable first impression.[2]

The children's new home was a short drive away, a couple of miles out of the city. Sketty Park House had been acquired by the council in 1931. It was a substantial Regency mansion dating from 1806 and had been assembled, in large part, from materials salvaged from an earlier Classical house built for the Morris family and demolished when the stench from nearby works forced a move to 'pastures green'.[3] After a month spent living under canvas at North Stoneham, it must have seemed overwhelming to the children. On the ground floor were a series of grand living rooms, all elegantly decorated. These rooms were clustered around a large reception hall which was dominated by an imposing staircase. On the first floor was a succession of bedrooms and bathrooms. These had been allocated to the girls. Behind the family accommodation were the somewhat less ornate servants' quarters. Here, long dimly lit corridors linked a big kitchen, a wash room and various store rooms and pantries. A narrow winding staircase led to garret rooms which were to house the boys. From the terrace in front of the house, it was possible to glimpse the broad sweep of Swansea bay. It was on this terrace that the committee gathered to welcome the children officially. The town's mayor, Councillor Richard Henry, received the new arrivals and said a few words of welcome through an interpreter. A gramophone player was produced and a record of Basque songs played.[4]

The intensity of the welcome in Swansea may have owed something to the fact that it was the home port of the celebrated seafarer 'Potato' Jones. Now styling himself Refugee Jones, he was still plying the seas off the northern Spanish coast, his trademark top hat always on his head, conveying women and children refugees from Santander. His vessel, the *Marie Llewellyn* had been renamed the *Kenwyl* in an attempt to confuse Franco's navy. At the same time as the refugees were settling into Sketty Park, the captain was arriving at St Nazaire with 1,500 refugees, remaining on the bridge for forty-eight hours. Even his own cabin was, he reported, crammed with refugees. 'Perhaps I'll be able to get in there myself for a while now.' Such acts of daring inspired others to play their part, even if their roles were somewhat less epic than that of rumbustious Captain Jones.[5]

The speed with which the whole project had been set up meant that the children had already been settled in Sketty Park for the best part of a week by the time the official fund-raising campaign got off the ground. Its launch shared headlines in the local press with the disappearance over the Pacific Ocean of Amelia Earhart, the aviation pioneer, and the news that Franco's capital, Burgos, had been bombed by Republican planes.[6] The mayor wrote to 600 organizations in Swansea appealing for financial help and setting out the daunting sums involved. The target amount, calculated to be sufficient to maintain one child, was set at 13s. 6d a week, significantly higher than the estimate used by the other colonies in Wales. Organizations contacted included churches and chapels, clubs and associations, schools and groups of employees, as well as prominent local citizens. Within a fortnight of its launch the mayor's fund stood at £220. 'We extend the hospitality of our ancient borough to innocent sufferers amongst the dependents of both conflicting parties', wrote the mayor in his appeal.

> Following the arrival of 80 children, it is not possible to fix a definite period during which the need will continue, but it is considered that the requirements should prudently be based on maintenance of the children for about 40 weeks. On this basis it is estimated that about £2,250 will be needed for adaptation, equipment and staffing of the home and for the maintenance and clothing of the children.[7]

There were eighty-four refugees, the youngest only five years old and the oldest seventeen. They were, for the most part, in a poor state. Filthy dirty, many of the children had bumps and wounds. A barber was called to improve their bedraggled appearance.

There were also cases of scabies and a single instance of typhoid that required admission to the isolation ward of the local cottage hospital.[8] More difficult to deal with than physical hurt were the psychological traumas suffered by the children. Many were distraught for the first two weeks of their stay in Swansea. The children's appearance made a deep impression on the young Rose Noriega who worked as an interpreter at the home. In an article in the *South Wales Evening Post* she recalled her first impressions:

> When I first set eyes on the children they were very slight indeed. They were all frail and frightened and many looked like skeletons. Many had their belongings wrapped up in pieces of cloth or in a cardboard box. For the first few weeks, they would scream and run for cover when they heard airplanes passing overhead because they thought that they would be bombed. They were all young and many cried for their mother.[9]

On one occasion, blankets went missing and were discovered in a makeshift shelter constructed in the grounds. Feeling too exposed in the home, some of the children had dug two tunnels like the entrance to an igloo. These tunnels had been camouflaged and made ready in case of an air raid. Rose Noriega recalls the discovery of the tunnels: 'Down I crawled. All the walls were lined with bricks taken from Cherry Grove and straw from the neighbouring farms.'[10]

In comparison with the ordeals of war, the problems the refugees faced at Sketty Park were unexceptional. One boy, falling from a tree, broke his arm. A girl, Margarita, fell ill with anaemia and had to go to hospital, 'a lovely hospital by the way'. One night there was an undesired visit from a man seen peering through the window of the room, causing the committee to put two guards outside and make a request for spotlights to be installed. The committee faced a delicate dilemma when it was discovered that one of the teenage boys had become sexually active with one of the girls. A potential scandal was averted by sending the boy back to Bilbao and the girl to Barcelona. There was also a 'disagreeable incident' with a dog that made the local papers. Begona Ballesteros recalls:

> Some of the estate workers gave us a very pretty dog. It was very kind, but it had the habit of returning to the neighbouring estate to chase cows which would run away. One day, the farmer shot him dead. We buried him in the garden of the estate and put flowers on his grave.[11]

Overwhelmingly, the children's recollections of their time in Sketty Park are happy ones. 'They treated us wonderfully', Amelia Fuentes recalls; 'the food was good, with butter, marmalade and milk.' There were endless cups of tea. Lunch was often soup with lentils and sometimes meat. At four, there was jam and bread and in the evening there was supper followed by milky coffee. The children's health improved and they began to put on weight.[12] They remember the visit of King George VI, which occurred shortly after their arrival. The children were allocated a vantage point for this Ruritanian spectacle, on the royal route to the Guildhall. That visit was the prelude to an extended summer holiday with plenty of outings to nearby beaches and regular day trips to the countryside. The Christmas celebrations that year were another highlight. Each child got presents from under a decorated tree. There were games and a traditional turkey dinner.

Each day had its own rhythm. To begin with, the time allocated to lessons was limited. There was an hour of lessons in the morning and two in the afternoon, plus an additional hour of voluntary English. By the time that Antonia became a teacher the school day had been extended. Lessons in basic mathematics and literacy were taught between 9 a.m. and midday, with further lessons between 2 and 4 o'clock. After this, the children were allowed to play. Bath time was restricted to the evening. Maria Fuentes recollects that the Basque government paid each teacher £1 10s. a week, and there were complaints because sometimes the money took time arriving. On Saturdays, there were chores in the morning. The girls would help clean the house and the boys worked in the gardens, but afterwards the children were free to play. The gardens at Sketty Park provided endless opportunities for the children to go exploring. The grounds were dotted with rhododendron bushes and there were pine trees to climb. There was a walled vegetable garden and a gothic 'belvedere', a folly that commanded fine views across the countryside.

Sometimes, on Sundays and bank holidays, there would be visitors from the town. The secretary of the appeal, the well-regarded Mr Saunders, and his wife and daughter were frequent visitors, as was D. R. Grenfell the MP for the Gower.[13] Townsfolk would often come with presents and spend almost the whole day with the children. Contributions were invited and there was a collection box in the hall.[14] Communication was difficult. The children spoke very little English, although even the youngest child had learned to say 'OK mister'. Beyond this, both parties had to get by with hand signals.[15] If the children had behaved themselves during the week, they might be allowed to go for a visit to local families. The teachers' training college also regularly entertained the girls for an afternoon. Antonia Lapera recalls being invited to a miner's house for tea. She could see that they did not have very much, but the little they did have was offered willingly: 'When you have nothing, you give it all. Not many well to do people visited the colony. Only the working class managed to find time to call in and leave money in the donation box.'

There were other visitors to the colony, merchant seamen from Basque ships who were running the blockade. Whenever they docked in Swansea to collect food and supplies for the tottering Republic, they would visit the colony. They would arrive laden with sweets and bearing news of last-ditch resistance to Franco. The press reported that one of the Spanish sailors gave an 'admirable talk' to the children. 'There was', he urged, 'a fine opportunity through exemplary conduct based on gratitude for hospitality, of helping future friendship between the two countries.'[16] The children placed great importance on visits from these mariners who provided a vital link with their homeland. For the sailors, the prospect of seeing one of the young *señoritas* who worked in the colony may also have played a small part in their keenness to keep in touch.[17]

Like all the colonies, Sketty Park received no financial support from the British government. The project would never have got off the ground without an initial pledge of £1,000 from Lord Davies and £500 from each of his sisters Margaret and Gwendoline. The list of subsequent contributors is evidence of the widespread support that the Basque refugees enjoyed, support that included, but went well beyond, the political Left. The Communist Party gave financial help, but so did the Boy Scouts movement and the Bible College of Wales. Swansea Rotary Club agreed to give £100 from their fete to the mayor's fund. The Market Traders' Association gave gifts of pulses, fruit and vegetables. Footwear came from local shopkeepers. Various items of bedding were made by Swansea Institute for the Blind. Collections were taken from those viewing the royal procession and money was collected on the sands. Donations came from libraries, hotels, insurance companies and greengrocers. The YMCA contributed regularly, so did the Co-operative Guild and Swansea Soroptimists. Many council departments organized collections, among them the office of the borough engineer, and the weights and measures department. The long list of those making donations of utensils, furniture, bedding and other household goods included several from the Spanish communities of Abercraf and Dowlais. There was a tidal wave of giving.[18]

The willingness of thousands of workers in the metal industries of south Wales to support the Spanish Republic was directly contrary to their own interests. Self-preservation demanded that many in the workforce should have welcomed a Nationalist victory. Continuing the fight threatened their livelihoods. After all, had Franco not gone out of his way to safeguard British commercial interests in Spain? Within days of his subduing the Basque country, British members of staff of the Orconera Iron Ore Company were allowed to return to their Bilbao headquarters. The British Embassy at Hendaye had been in regular contact with Franco and permission was granted to the company by the Generalissimo personally for shipments of ore to Wales to be resumed with immediate effect. But if Franco expected any gratitude for his largesse, he received precious little from the conurbations of south Wales. Swansea trade unionists, who had already contributed £100 to the national campaign, gave the mayor's fund an additional £50. Their secretary, Mr Joe Davies, said that he anticipated that trade union branches could contribute a further £20 a fortnight, 'enough to sponsor an appreciable number of children'. Tin plate workers in Llansamlet gave 10s. every week. As elsewhere in Wales, there was also the unfailing support of the South Wales Miners' Federation. Other contributions came from quarry workers, offices and workingmen's clubs. Workplace deductions of at least a penny a week were suggested for all trade union members, officials expressing the hope that this example would be matched by a similar scheme from the Chamber of Trade.[19]

The cause of the Basque children found fervent support amongst the adherents of Welsh Nonconformity. Lists of contributors published each week provide evidence of some quite exceptional giving from the various denominations. The mayor's fund is heavy with the names of Bethel and Zion, Salem and Beulah. From the outset one Congregational chapel guaranteed to 'adopt' a child at the cost of 13s. 6d a week. Several others promised to devote a monthly retiring collection to this 'worthy service'. One such collection at Trinity Calvinistic Methodist Chapel in Park Street raised the enormous sum of £11. The Quakers, always amongst the most radical in outlook, were particularly active, promising to sponsor a child and donating equipment.

In Swansea, the Basque Children's Appeal was very much a civic project. Sketty Park had been brought into being following a meeting convened by the mayor and attended by representatives of various local organizations and Alan Collingridge of the National Joint Committee. The borough estate agent, D. Ivor Saunders, was the fund's honorary secretary and donations were collected in the Guildhall by the county treasurer, Mr R. A. Wetherall. The colony seems to have been well staffed and professionally run. Rose Noriega, who was born in Swansea of Spanish parents, was recruited through a newspaper advertisement and had to undergo an interview and written examination. The home employed six auxiliaries, two laundry women, two Spanish-speaking teachers and a cook. One of the teachers, 24-year-old Maria Lusia Fuentes, had come to Sketty Park with her two nephews. Another woman, the wife of an exiled Basque seafarer from Lekeito, volunteered to work without pay in the kitchen. Like the other colonies in Wales, Sketty Park could also draw on an earlier wave of Spanish settlers. As well as Rose, there was Tini Aleman (Augustina Lorenzo Funcia), who had come from Spain with her parents in 1909. Orphaned at the age of twelve, she was fostered by the Aleman family who were in business near the port. She often interpreted in court for the Spanish community, especially for seafarers. When the children arrived at Sketty Park she volunteered to help.[20]

The two sisters from Bilbao, Antonia and Lola shared a room. Their duties began at 7 o'clock when they would prepare *sopas de leche*, a breakfast of coffee, milk and bread. Antonia was given a job as a general carer, but early on she developed backache and found it difficult to carry out some of her duties. This weakness was seized upon by another worker at the home who had taken a dislike to Antonia from the moment of her arrival. She reported Antonia to the committee who decided that as she was unable to do her job she should leave Sketty Park.

Desolate and tearful, Antonia took refuge in a cafe in the port of Swansea. The welcome she received there was very friendly, with many of the customers insisting on buying her cups of tea. Amongst these customers was a Basque seafarer who recognized Antonia. He was the captain of the *Aherri Mendi*, he was also Antonia's knight in shining armour. What, he wanted to know, was she doing in that cafe? Did she not realize that it was the local pick-up place for sailors? This revelation increased Antonia's torment. She poured her heart out to the captain and he promised to do what he could to settle matters with those in charge at Sketty Park.

The captain was as good as his word. He negotiated Antonia's return to the colony. But when she returned she was not alone. The crew of the *Aherri Mendi* had made her a present of a young Alsatian dog named Acherri. The dog became the mascot and friend of practically all the children and staff. However, there were two sisters in the colony who, on medical grounds, had had their hair cut very short. Whenever the dog saw them he would snarl as though he was about to attack. The situation became intolerable and Antonia reluctantly decided to sell her dog. The buyer, she remembers, was a footballer who played for Swansea Town.

The mayor and borough council, having established the home, effectively handed over day-to-day responsibility to those who worked there. The committee concerned itself primarily with fund-raising and the children saw its members only on social occasions, or if there was some emergency. The running of the colony was entrusted for the most part to a group of five Spanish or Welsh-Hispanic women. This was a style of management that was not found in the other colonies in Wales. Almost inevitably, there were some tensions between individuals. To some extent, these were personal, but they also mirrored the political and religious divisions in the Basque country. Alone amongst the Welsh colonies, the children were encouraged to attend mass on Sundays. The older boys resisted but most of the girls and younger boys did go. At least one of the teachers at Sketty Park was a supporter of Franco's Nationalists and when the Republican government fell she decided to return home.[21] Her departure provided an opportunity for Antonia. She was promoted to teacher status and for five hours a day taught the children basic mathematics and literacy.

However, time was running out for the Swansea colony. Money was starting to dry up and the storm clouds of war were gathering across Europe. The colony was almost exactly a year old when the decision was taken that all those who had families still alive should go back home. Wherever possible, contact with parents had been maintained, mail was regularly received and the children followed closely the tragic events in their homeland. Most of the children were reportedly delighted to go back. Many of the older boys said they intended to join the Republican forces which were still fighting against Franco. In June 1938, Sketty Park closed and the remaining children were transferred to Birkenhead and other colonies. Most eventually went back to Franco's Spain.

Antonia did not return home with them. She found employment with the former ambassador for Spain, working at the Spanish Institute in Kensington and at his country residence near Maidenhead. There, she cooked for various exiled leaders including Charles de Gaulle and the former President Negrín. Lola was with her, working as a maid. In her spare time, Antonia sang with a Basque children's choir and it was at a concert in the Albert Hall that she met a young Republican officer. He became her husband in 1943 and a year later a son, Pedro, was born. Fear of arrest meant that Antonia and her husband did not return to Spain until 1959. By then, the family had put down deep roots in London. The house that she and her husband bought in 1949 is still Antonia's home. It is not very far from her sister Lola.

9 'THE BEST PART OF MY LIFE'

OLD COLWYN, beside the sea and in the shelter of mountains, has long been a haven for those seeking to recover health and happiness. Like its more brazen sisters, Abergele and Colwyn Bay, the town owed its prosperity to the flood of holidaymakers who arrived each summer by railway from the industrial conurbations. To these visitors, in the summer of 1937, were added twenty young Basque refugees.

The north Wales colony had its genesis in a single paragraph in a Colwyn Bay newspaper. A short article on an inside page, sandwiched between items on the Pier Pavilion concerts and the bowling results, quoted the appeal by the omnipresent Lord Davies to support the Welsh fund for the Basque children. Then it asked: 'Is there no organization in Colwyn Bay which would endeavour to house and feed some of the 4,000 Basque children who have come over to this country as refugees?'[1] The response was swift. A meeting was held in the town's council chambers. Forty representatives from all over north Wales met, with the aim of 'succouring and housing Basque children and contributing to their maintenance until they have been adopted'.[2]

The momentum behind the Basque refugee appeal sprang directly from an earlier campaign to send ambulances to Spain. The organizational and fund-raising structures were already in place and an Aid Spain shop had opened in Colwyn Bay. Initially, at least, the Welsh Ambulance for Spain Fund and the North Wales Basque Children's Home shared a committee, with Mr Rowland Bird acting as secretary of both organizations. Money raised at public meetings was expected to be split equally between the two groups. The ambulance appeal had been enormously successful, raising enough money to purchase a specially built, fully equipped vehicle that was sent to Spain with a dedicated driver and full medical team. As a fund-raising exercise, the Welsh ambulance appeal had definite advantages. First, it was undeniably non-partisan. As a humanitarian campaign, its purchase enjoyed support across the political spectrum. Also, it helped that the ambulance cost £500, a finite target that gave a sharper focus to fund-raising. In a remarkably short time the money was collected and a state-of-the-art ambulance left for Spain in April 1937, camouflaged in blue, brown and green with a *draig goch* (red dragon) on its bonnet. At the wheel was John Williams-Hughes, a journalist from Anglesey.[3]

This charitable, cross-party approach was maintained in the appeal for the Basque children's home. The local committee was unambiguous about its motivation: 'on humanitarianism alone is the home launched; no other issue'.[4] Leaflets emphasized that the project was for the relief of suffering and their appeal for money invoked the name of the duchess of Atholl as well as MPs of every political hue. It also made a point of saying that it was asking for help only until the children could be returned to their homes and parents. Letters to the press stressed time and again the non-political aspects of the venture. 'It remains for the rest of us to do our bit, remembering that we do it not because we are Socialists or Tories, but because: In as much as ye have done it unto one of the least of these my children, ye have done it unto me.'[5] Colonel O. A. Evans, who presided at several of the fund-raising events, never missed an opportunity to stress that there was no political flavour whatsoever in the home.

Such reassurance was needed. Accusations were made that the committee formed to run Rooftree House was little more than a cover for ideological intrigues.[6] But, if these men were indeed fellow travellers, then they came with impeccable bourgeois credentials. The president, Henry Parry, was mayor of Colwyn Bay and a JP. He had just completed thirty-seven years as a station foreman working on the LMS railway. The chairman, Alfred Lynn, was active in the scouting movement; he had become district commissioner in 1930 and remained in this role for eighteen years. The treasurer, Mr J. M. Evans, was the manager of Lloyds Bank in the town. Several aldermen, a retired army colonel and a glut of councillors all lent their support. None are obvious candidates for the Leninist category of 'useful idiot'. On the contrary, there are indications of some nervousness about being considered overtly political. Some of the internal correspondence concerns a dispute over the failure to mention in leaflets 'the heroic work of Leah Manning . . . the very person who evacuated the children'. This was explained by those responsible for the leaflets as a simple mistake which would be put right. But the accusation that members were deliberately avoiding controversy struck a raw nerve. 'As to political bias, we have none. In a matter like this, we are in it from humanitarian principles alone.'[7]

Suitable accommodation for the refugees was secured at Rooftree House in Meiriadog Road, a former school for girls. A large, empty building near the centre of the small town and within sight of the sea, the house was judged ideal to house the small group of children who had been allocated to north Wales. The newspapers reported that 'Miss Bird, owner of Rooftree School, has shown her humanity by letting her house at what might be called commercially a ridiculous rent'.[8] Arrangements for the tenancy of Rooftree had been completed by the end of June, but it was a full month before the youngsters arrived. In the meantime, the mood in some quarters had turned sour. Just prior to the children's arrival, the press had been full of the 'deplorable incident elsewhere in Wales' and this coverage had generated some hostile letters in the local papers. A Colwyn Bay resident, G. J. Mayor, described the project as 'a fine example of mistaken kindness'. He was, he said, disturbed by the violent escapades of refugees elsewhere and felt that the town 'already has its hands pretty full controlling its own wayward youngsters'. Moreover, 'Franco had plenty of places where these young people would find comfort and safety'.[9] Correspondence between members of the committee confirms the impact that the incident at Brechfa had on local opinion. One internal memo written shortly after the disturbances reported that: 'Hostility was in the town owing to the Brechfa outbreak and everyone windy about their cars and windows etc, but they are coming round now and taking to the children better.'[10]

In response to such fears, the Basque Children's Committee launched an immediate exercise in damage limitation. Their spokesman, Allen Arnaud, was contrite about events at Brechfa. He reassured the local community that the children living in their midst would be 'well behaved and delightful'. Old Colwyn would be sent only quiet, younger boys and girls, he promised. 'Children of the Brechfa type would be immediately returned.' This defensive, even timorous, tone was echoed by the secretary of the local committee Mr J. Wesley Jones. He invited local people to visit the home where they would see for themselves that 'these little girls and boys are not the ruffians some imagine but normal little children torn from their home'.[11]

An apologetic undercurrent pervades much of the discussion of the refugees' arrival, as though it was necessary to decouple the children's plight from the chaotic struggle in Spain. The children, it was stressed time and again, were innocent and helpless sufferers, however much one might deplore the quarrels in their homeland. Compassion should be extended to the children whether political sympathies lay with the Spanish government or the insurgents. 'No man with a heart should refuse to succour a homeless child merely because its parents are dyed-in-the-wool Reds or any other colour', wrote one correspondent.[12] Defenders of the refugees also had to deal with the pervasive sentiment that charity should begin (and probably end) at home. One letter tackles this issue head on:

> We are told that we have poor in our own country. This condition is also to be deplored and, whenever possible alleviated, but where in our own country have we children who move in very danger of their lives, whose homes are burned and who do not know whether their parents are alive or dead, who have no one to whom to turn in their dark hour of deep distress?[13]

So, on a Friday evening in early August, nine boys and eleven girls disembarked at Colwyn Bay railway station. On arrival at

Rooftree each child was allocated a bed and on each bed was a toy. Such impossible luxury brought little cries of delight from children accustomed to sleeping on straw. As promised, the children were young: the oldest was twelve years old and the youngest six. They were, by all accounts, particularly well behaved and respectful. The community seemed to be instantly won over. Comments from local people who met the children express universal approval: 'I fell in love with their sweet faces, in fact a lump came to my throat'; 'They are made to be cared for not bombed'; 'The loveliest of little Spanish children'; 'How happy they seem when anybody looks interested in them'.

Money was never plentiful. The speed at which the colony was set up meant that there were questions over whether the project could be sustained. The urgency of the need was best summed up by one concise public appeal: 'You live in north Wales, these children are your guests and your charge.'[14] Yet, as initial hesitancies were overcome, the treasurer could say in his September report that matters were on a more even keel: 'Things at Rooftree are running well. We are tackling the finances now. Delighted when work such as this prospered the way it has done – beyond my expectations. For difficulties have been no difficulties when they have been met.'[15]

The local Spanish Aid committee had made over £60 in door-to-door collections and a well-attended public meeting in July had elicited promises to sponsor six children. Rydal public school agreed to pay 10s. a week for an indefinite period and, not to be outdone, the girls' school, Penrhos College, promised a weekly contribution of £1, enough to sponsor two children. To help with any shortfall there was an endless round of jumble sales in the Co-op hall, collections in local chapels, or visits to local carnivals. One typical memorandum recorded a successful visit to the Toc H show in Caernarfon: 'The children have gone over there with matron, making an absolute hit with the natives.'[16]

Despite such generosity, the north Wales colony never secured the sort of sustained giving that would guarantee a regular monthly income. It lacked civic sponsorship or financial backing from a trades union. Rooftree was, therefore, more dependent on charitable giving and was consequently at the mercy of fickle public opinion. To add to the difficulties, it was never going to be easy raising funds, or raising consciousness, in seaside resorts catering for holidaymakers. Anniversary celebrations, receptions and concert parties might raise enough to cover running costs for another week or so, but it was a precarious way of life.

The degree to which the children earned their own keep was escalating. In January at a concert held at the YMCA the children sang songs in Basque, Spanish and English. The press reported that, 'a doll song by four little Basque girls was loudly applauded'.[17] At a carnival to celebrate the first anniversary of the children's arrival the girls gave an exhibition of skipping. The previous month there had been an 'at home' attended by the mayoress, where the children sold flowers and home-made articles. The event raised just over £14.[18]

Old Colwyn was the designated home for the whole of north Wales, an area from Caernarfon to Chester, but in practice almost all the contributions needed to keep the home open had to be raised in the borough. The financial situation was insecure throughout the life of the home, as the aptly named committee member Mr Welcome Mitchell made clear:

> The support given to the Old Colwyn home, which is the only one in north Wales, from the north Wales districts generally, with the exception of course of the Borough of Colwyn Bay, has been spasmodic. The money we have received from sources outside Colwyn Bay has only amounted to a small proportion of the sum required for the upkeep of the home.[19]

As well as gifts of money, the home had other needs. An urgent appeal went out for boys' trousers – several of the lads owned only the pair in which they stood up. There was also a shortage of shoes, blankets, nightdresses and pyjamas. Furniture was in short supply, particularly chests of drawers and lockers. Supporters loaned or parted with a good deal of their own furniture to equip the home. Leaflets begged for donations: 'There remains the question of furniture. I understand there are sufficient beds but chairs, a rug or two and bedroom appurtenances are still required. A visit to attics and lumber rooms would seem to be indicated.'[20]

Those first weeks were portrayed in the press as a kind of idyll for the children. They played in the garden, 'the girls sitting in a group singing little Spanish songs and dancing some of their native dances'.[21] Lessons took place in the morning, beginning at 9.15, and started with the children giving 'personal impressions of anything they have noticed on the previous day. This is sometimes very illuminating and their active little minds are quick to pick up items of interest and beauty in this wonderful new life that has somehow opened up around them.'[22] The curriculum was traditional, concentrating on the three Rs, singing, drill, drawing and handicraft. Afternoons were spent bathing in the sea or basking in the sunshine.

The 'little inmates' were taught to say three English phrases in clear English: 'I like Colwyn Bay', 'You are very kind' and 'Thank you very much'. This was 'so that they may express in some small measure the gratitude and happiness they feel'.[23] In the evening, if the dinner was especially good, the girls would insist on kissing all those who had served them. Seven of the children had no idea of their true birthdays so one Friday was selected for a joint celebration. This un-birthday party was an occasion of much merriment. The guest of honour, the mayor, Mr Parry, made a speech. There was a huge cake and games until bedtime. A collection taken after the meal was sent to the local hospital where one of the children, Antonio, had recently been treated. The local newspapers reported that the children were growing in health, had adapted well to their new environment and were quite happy.

However, no amount of warmth and understanding could magic away the horrors that the children had experienced in their homeland. A spectacular sunset was enough to trigger sobbing and terror as tiny children relived bombardments and slaughter. Mr Welcome Mitchell described the 'nervous fear' of children who had seen their homes bombed and who had then been 'rushed off to a country where all the people and their language were strange to them'.[24] Every one of the children in Rooftree carried fears about what was happening to their families in Spain. Each was troubled by dread. The father of one child in the colony had been sentenced by the Franco authorities to thirty years' imprisonment for being a supporter of the Basque government. Two brothers of another child were prisoners in a rebel camp. Their house had been destroyed and their mother left with six children whom she was unable to feed properly. The first anniversary of the bombing of Guernica coincided with a fund-raising event in Old Colwyn. The committee in London had asked that the children observe a two-minute silence to commemorate the event, but at Rooftree the massacre went unmarked. 'To do so', wrote Wesley Jones, 'would invite sadness and bitterness.'[25]

The matron of Rooftree, Miss Onzarde, was a British-born Basque. She had arrived at the home accompanied by her widowed mother who had fled Spain earlier that summer. In addition there were two teachers, one local and the other Spanish, and two helpers, both Spanish speakers. To this core was added a profusion of volunteers. A woman gave up her holiday to work as a maid in the home. A carpenter came in for an hour twice a week. The resident cook, Mrs Harsent, was unpaid. Doctors, dentists and the district nurse gave their services free.

There is no doubting the warmth of the welcome shown to the youngsters by many in the wider community. Captain Perry of Llandudno took all twenty children on a 'delightful' cruise to the Menai Straits aboard his steamship, the *Lady Orme*. The Odeon at Colwyn Bay and the wonderfully named Supreme Picture House in Old Colwyn gave the youngsters free showings of films. The local boy scouts took the children bathing and for country rambles. The presence of the Basque children provided an opportunity to express practical kindness towards the innocent and the helpless.

A friendship that sprang up that summer has remained constant ever since. A local girl, Elsie Dodd, became firm friends with one of the refugees Nati Gonzalez. Elsie was then a 16-year-old laundry worker; she and her friend, Doreen Jones, would spend all their spare time at Rooftree going for walks and playing with Nati and her brother Jose Luis. Today, Elsie still lives in north Wales and has clear memories of how a friendship which stretches back seventy years began:

> To me, the Basque children were extremely exotic. I had never met anyone foreign before. I went to visit them at the school and we communicated as best we could, and were helped by their two teachers, who could speak

English. They were very friendly so I went to visit as much as I could. Some of the children would sometimes come for tea at my parents' house and they were allowed to go to the cinema for free on Saturday mornings. The only time I lost touch with Nati was during the Second World War. She was back in Spain then and communication was impossible.[26]

The man who did most to bring Rooftree into being was a dental technician who lived in Mochdre, Douglas Hyde. 'Mr Hyde's efforts for these children', wrote the local paper, 'have been so enormous that they cannot be measured by the ordinary standards of work'. Hyde was a man of huge energy and charisma, capable of inspiring tremendous loyalty. When he moved to Northwich shortly after the children arrived, the local paper lamented that he 'would not see the fruits of his own servings'.[27] In his autobiography Hyde described the years he spent in north Wales as, 'not only the most memorable and personally satisfying, but the best part of my life'. His brief account of his time in north Wales was written thirteen years after the children had dispersed. By this time, Hyde had undergone a remarkable personal conversion. As a boy growing up in Bristol, he had listened to soap-box orators on Clifton Downs, speakers who had included the Rhondda firebrand Lewis Jones. He had become a convinced Marxist and in 1928, aged seventeen, he had joined the Communist Party. It was the start of a political journey that would lead him eventually to become the news editor on the party newspaper, the *Daily Worker*, a paper of some influence in the 1940s, with a circulation of 120,000. Then, after twenty years in the forefront of the party, he and his wife sensationally abandoned communism entirely to join the Roman Catholic Church, captivated by the neo-medievalist theories of Belloc and Chesterton.[28]

Hyde's belief in the rightness of the anti-Franco campaign was, at the time, entirely genuine and he applied himself unstintingly to harnessing support for that cause. But his genuine purpose went beyond the immediate task. Behind the torrent of meetings, film shows, street collections, the purchase of ambulances and provision for refugees there was always an ideological imperative. He was the Communist Party organizer for north Wales. For many years, by his own admission, he was also the only party member between Chester and Holyhead. Yet, by 1937, the party had developed sufficiently to justify the formation of a district committee and had branches in Bethesda, Wrexham and the Vale of Conway. This growth was largely due to the impact of the war in Spain.

Hyde had been the channel for much of the frenzied campaigning across the region since the outbreak of the conflict. By the spring of 1937, there was scarcely a corner of north Wales where he had not proclaimed the gospel of solidarity with the Spanish Republic. Meetings had been held in chapels, dance halls and picture houses from Holyhead to Flint. It was claimed that two or three meetings were being held every day, with the collection at each meeting averaging £20.[29] *The Defence of Madrid*, a documentary film often shown at these gatherings, made a great impact and where possible the footage was augmented by speakers with first-hand experience of the conflict. In Wrexham, the speaker was Gordon Davies, who had driven an ambulance in the government zone. His speech emphasized that the fighting was 'not really a civil war but an invasion by international fascism'.[30] At another public meeting in a village near Bethesda, there was an auction of a hat worn by a Spanish militia man. The successful bidder passed up an unopened pay packet. The same happened with bids for a second item, a militia girl's scarf. 'Both went to quarryman earning pitifully little. Similar sacrifices were later made at later meetings by miners, agricultural workers, railwaymen and other low-paid workers.'[31]

The response at these gatherings sometimes resembled a Revivalist meeting. After a showing of the film in Bangor's Penrhyn Hall, at which the collection raised £40 on top of the admission fee, there was a spontaneous call for a committee to be set up 'for the provision of comforts for the defenders of Madrid'. A Bangor branch of Aid Spain was duly established to campaign and collect goods and money. The press reported that 'all present voiced the feeling that widespread sympathy exists for the people in Spain'.[32]

Occasionally at such meetings recruits came forward to volunteer for the International Brigade. One such volunteer, from the slate-mining village of Penygroes, was George Fretwell; he was killed at the battle of Jarama in February 1937. In a conversation after the public meeting in Rhosllannerchrugog, a 27-year-old miner, Tom Jones, asked Arthur Horner: 'what are the possibilities of getting to Spain'? He was told to visit the party's headquarters in London. Within weeks he had illegally entered Spain via France and served with the brigade for two years, seeing action in Brunete and Teruel. Captured after the battle on the river Ebro, he was held in Franco's jails until March 1939.[33] 'The Communist's appeal to idealism is direct and audacious', wrote Hyde. 'They say if you make mean little demands upon people you will get a mean little response, which is all you deserve, but if you big demands on them you will get an historic response.'[34]

A point was reached when Hyde had held a meeting in every town, village and hamlet in north Wales and it became clear to him that a new type of humanitarian appeal was required if his strategic mission was to be carried forward. The arrival of the Basque child refugees provided him with just what he needed and he immediately threw himself into the appeal for a Basque Children's Home.

Hyde's subsequent best-selling autobiography, *I Believed,* became a set text for cold warriors in the 1950s. But Hyde was always more than just a crude McCarthyite. In his way, he was a tireless idealist – quixotic, idiosyncratic and utopian. Towards the end of his life, he managed to reconcile his religious impulse with progressive politics, but the record of his work in establishing Rooftree stems from a time when his hostility to Stalinist ruthlessness was at its zenith. It was written with an eye for ideological point scoring and this makes the post-communist Hyde a hostile witness. In this incarnation, he claimed that attempts by the comrades to agitate on behalf of Republican Spain were little more than a cynical ruse. As for the children, he was delighted that his own inclinations and the party line coincided. 'I fell in love with them at once', he wrote, but nonetheless the refugees were 'just an excuse for yet another campaign against war and fascism, an excuse for making new sympathisers and, one hoped, new Party members too'.

The appearance of communists on a platform alongside Liberals in Caernarfon, or their providing speakers for meetings sponsored by the Church in Wales, formed part of a deliberate strategy of innocence by association.[35] Working with Welsh MPs like the Liberal, Megan Lloyd George, in a non-partisan ambulance campaign increased the party's visibility and brought it political kudos. The approach of the Communist Party of Great Britain (CPGB) at the time was to inch its way towards that glorious day when it would take its place in a Popular Front with other 'democratic parties' opposed to the National Government and non-intervention.

Machiavellian manoeuvring should not obscure a simple truth. The vast majority of those who took on the responsibility of looking after, feeding and clothing the children at Rooftree were motivated solely by compassion. They knew that the proper place for the children would be at home with their parents, but if the refugees had been left at home they would have been living in dreadful squalor, or would perhaps have been killed. The task of caring for the children was not a light one but lacking any real understanding of what conditions were like in Franco's Spain and without assurances that the children would be safe, they were not prepared to surrender their responsibility. In a letter of appreciation to the north Wales committee, the Basque government delegate in London, Señor José de Lisaro, wrote:

> The great work you have done in restoring these war-tortured youngsters to healthy normality and in caring for them these many months is a matter upon which I find it difficult to express our full feelings. May I simply say, on behalf of my Government and myself, that you have rendered not only to the Basque people but to humanity itself a great service, and that we look forward to the time when, once more restored to Euzkadi, under conditions of an honourable peace, we may be able to show some measure of our indebtedness.[36]

In May 1938, exactly a year after the arrival of the children in this country, the first refugees from Rooftree went home. After months of correspondence, two brothers aged six and eight were returned to their parents in San Sebastian. Their mother, sending her thanks to those who had cared for her children, commented on how well her sons looked and how happy they had been in Old Colwyn. Over the summer months a further twelve children returned to Spain and another joined her brother in the colony in Margate. By the end of September the number remaining at Rooftree had dwindled to five. The Basque Children's Committee in London, desperate to secure sufficient accommodation for the 1,500 orphaned children still under its care, wanted to keep Rooftree open. It dispatched Eleanor Rathbone MP to try to persuade the local committee to accept children transferred from other centres. But raising the necessary funds was proving increasingly difficult and so, on 14 October 1938, the North Wales Basque Children's Home closed its doors. The remaining children were transferred to the colony at Leicester. The end, when it came, was restrained and unfussy. There was no formal farewell ceremony in Meiriadog road, instead the home's benefactors gathered at the railway station to say goodbye to children whose lives they had shared for over a year.

Saving the lives of the children was the only object for the band of helpers and, to this end, they gave freely of their time, money and affection. If there was a political message, it was an uncomplicated one, that the plight of the children of Spain was a foretaste of what might happen to the children of any other nation. The quiet decency that sustained the community at Rooftree is perhaps best illustrated by an anonymous fragment written under the title 'Reply to criticism':

> A country, blessed as we know our own to be, seeks to share its bounty. Because these are children just like the children who brighten our own homes, because they have suffered in a way that we trust our own children may never know. As a thank offering for our peaceful homes, let us not 'pass by on the other side'. This country has ever given shelter to the less fortunate, so we take them in and shelter them from the storm, giving them simple, wholesome days and wonderful memories of this land. May seeds be sown, which in future years shall bear fruit and help to build the ideals of peace and harmony amongst all nations.[37]

10 FAULT LINES

'Whether the British ruling class are wicked or merely stupid is one of the most difficult questions of our time.'
George Orwell (1943)

DESPITE SUPPORTIVE HEADLINES in the *South Wales Argus* declaring that the refugees 'have many friends at Caerleon', not quite everyone welcomed the 'Basque bairns'. On Friday 2 July 1937, a meeting had been held at Newport town hall. Its purpose was to put the seal of approval on the use of Cambria House. A working party of nine was to be chosen, who would collaborate with other local committees to oversee the running of a home for fifty children. The board seeking approval was a model of civic propriety consisting of two aldermen, three clergymen, the headmistress of the local girls' school and two JPs.

First, however, Alderman C. T. Clissitt JP had a question: 'Does the necessity exist for the effort you are asking us to make?' the alderman wanted to know. He also asked whether the National Joint Committee for Spanish Relief was actively working for the repatriation of the children to Spain, 'so that they could enjoy the homes from which they came'. He was asking this question, he explained, not because he was out of sympathy with the children, but because he thought the council should stop hearing only one side. He then read an extract from the Catholic newspaper, the *Universe*.

> Bilbao, freed from Red domination, is anxiously awaiting the return of the 4,000 children now scattered over various parts of England. Parents forced by threats to part

> with sons and daughters want them back. The National authorities want them. Homes await them, food, clothing, and, what they cannot possibly get in a foreign country however friendly, their natural surroundings and all that these surroundings imply.

Mr Alan Collingridge, representing the London office of the National Joint Committee for Spanish Relief (NJCSR), stressed that the children had been accepted out of humanitarian not political concerns. As for the question of repatriation, he said: 'if the parents want their children back and it is safe to send them back then they will be sent back'. Alderman Clissitt was seemingly alone in his scepticism. The Anglican rector of St Mary's, Father Colbert, spoke of the splendid work already done and 'the consideration given to all sensibilities'. Professor H. A. Marquand, representing the lord mayor of Cardiff's committee, emphasized the broad political and religious support for Cambria House, including that from the Roman Catholic Church. 'We are maintaining the tradition of our country', he said, 'which has always stood for offering shelter to the unfortunate.'[1]

The attitude of the Catholic Church to the evacuation was at best equivocal. It had lent its support to the initial emergency evacuation plan, but it increasingly regarded the whole venture with suspicion. Swiftly, its misgivings hardened into outright opposition. Nevertheless, out of common humanity, it did what it could to relieve suffering. More than fifty children with religious backgrounds were given accommodation with Catholic families in Wales and, for a short time, fifteen children were reportedly accommodated in an orphanage in the Cathays district of Cardiff run by the Sisters of Nazareth.[2] In north Wales, the Church arranged for a group of thirty-one Basques to join the Liverpool diocese's camping holiday. They joined 200 other children under canvas at Towyn. They were all 'little dears', according to the sister in charge. 'They have been perfectly fine in camp. We have had not a scrap of trouble with them. With the exception of one or two, they have no idea where their parents are.'[3]

The hierarchy of the Catholic Church was plainly and fervently in support of Franco. It condemned as 'unnatural and tragic' the alliance between the Basques and the Madrid leftists.[4]

It portrayed the evacuation of the children as at best a rash and foolish plan and at worst a devious scheme to blacken the image of the Nationalist forces. The editor of the *Catholic Herald* newspaper, Michael de la Bedoyere, had opposed from the start the 'unjust exiling' from their families of the 4,000 children, claiming that they were sent to Britain for no other purpose than to foster sympathy for the Valencia government. Throughout the summer of 1937, the paper ran articles and photographs portraying Franco's forces as liberators and upholders of the European Christian tradition. Week by week, it contrasted the popular enthusiasm felt for the Nationalists with the cruelty and hunger inflicted on the population in Republican areas.

The fall of Bilbao released the Church from a profound dilemma. It had been obliged out of simple Christian benevolence to offer succour to fellow Catholics who were refugees. Once the Basque country had been 'liberated', that obligation was lifted. The children should go home at once. From July onwards, the *Herald* was loud in its demands that the children be sent back. Under the headline 'Basques ask for children's return', it claimed that every day it was receiving appeals for repatriation from parents and guardians. The paper printed ten of the letters, all of which portrayed Franco's occupation of the territory around Bilbao as a release from Red oppression and starvation. All pleaded for their children to be allowed to return to Spain. The manoeuvres of the Catholic newspapers were, said the *Daily Worker*, 'a vile press campaign being waged to have the Basque kiddies sent back to rebel territory'.[5]

The ideological battle lines were drawn. For both sides, the war in Spain was splendidly clear cut, a clash between light and darkness. The Catholic Church regarded the Bilbao exodus as an enforced exile and it seized upon it as a weapon in a greater struggle. The archbishop of Westminster, Cardinal Hinsley, likened the war to 'a furious battle between Christian civilization and the most cruel Paganism that has ever darkened the world'.[6] Pope Pius XII, in a radio broadcast, spoke of his 'bitter pain in seeing so many innocent children taken from their homes and carried off to faraway lands, often with such dangers of apostasy and perversion'.[7] The refugees, said the *Catholic Times*, could be 'divided between Catholics and hooligans

. . . with the Catholics behaving themselves and the hooligans a danger to life and property; they furnish an apt picture of what is happening in Spain today'.[8]

The Catholic Church took its place in a coalition of groups which were implacably opposed to the whole mission. Fervent supporters of Franco objected to the arrival of the refugees because they saw the children themselves as conscripts in an enemy coalition, 'potentially murderous little wretches'. For them, the evacuation was nothing more than an exercise in leftist propaganda. Ardent Nationalists were not alone in this view. It was on the grounds that the arrival of the Basque children was an ideological manoeuvre that the Save the Children Fund had withdrawn its support from the evacuation. The charity claimed that the NJCSR was politically motivated and that children should not be separated from their parents.[9]

The right-wing press was remorseless in its portrayal of all Republicans as 'Red scum' and those who supported them as 'our horde of pacifists, sentimentalists and security mongers who still mouth the Geneva gibberish on behalf of Red gangsters'.[10] The extraordinary ferocity of the language used by the Northcliffe press in particular against those whom they opposed is startling. Isolated examples of bad behaviour and outbreaks of trouble, like the incident at Brechfa, were used as ammunition in the battle to discredit the 'Socialists, pinks and pacifists' and justify demands for the refugees to go home. The letters pages echoed the pro-Franco line. A common theme was that the Republic had allowed communists and anarchists to run amok. Dormant prejudices, depicting all Spaniards as untamed cut-throats, were revived. Wild worries were cultivated that the children would spread trachoma, an infectious eye disease.[11] It was also argued that their presence might spread political contagion, triggering a Red victory in some future election: 'innocent children being turned into Christ hating little communists'. There was angry criticism at the 'profligate sum' that the committee had fixed for the maintenance of each refugee. At 10s. a week it was considerably more than was given to the children of the British unemployed.

Eminent British supporters of Franco set up a Spanish Children Repatriation Committee to campaign for the refugees to be 'returned to the place from which they came'. The Basque

Children's Committee, they argued was deliberately obstructing the children's return to Spain on political grounds. The repatriation committee claimed to be a humanitarian and non-political organization. However, the membership scarcely indicates impartiality. Its chairman, Sir Arnold Wilson MP, had been described as, 'an admirer of Hitler and an unscrupulous propagandist'.[12] Other leading members included Sir Nairne Stewart-Sandeman MP, a founding member of the Friends of Nationalist Spain, Sir Henry Page Croft MP, who 'objected to the feeding of Red children', and Lady Londonderry, the well-connected political hostess and promoter of appeasement. In an interview with the *Manchester Guardian* Sir Nairne offered some befuddled advice:

> I don't mind telling you that I am on the Repatriation Committee about these little Basque devils and it is difficult to get them back. Don't pay a penny towards the upkeep of these Basques because not a single member of the Committee is going to put up the money to keep them. They are a pretty expensive cup of tea.[13]

By August 1938, the political fault lines were apparent to all. The remaining refugees had to struggle against a version of events that depicted them as adherents of a defeated cause. Voices were raised asking why the children should not return to a country that was now largely at peace. Their continued presence was increasingly regarded as an anomaly.

In Wales, unlike in Britain as a whole, condemnation of the Republic was almost beyond the pale. Expressions of support for Franco's cause were not politically acceptable, except on the very fringes of Welsh society. But such conventions did not apply to the greatest of all the business dynasties in Wales, the Bute family. The family had substantial commercial interests in Spain and with their powerful voices and deep coffers, they did what they could to advance Franco's cause. The third marquess had been one of the richest men in Britain and bequeathed to his son ownership of much of Cardiff and a considerable fortune derived from the mining and export of coal. Augusta Stuart, the wife of the fourth marquess, was, like her husband, a committed Catholic. She was also a zealous supporter of Franco.

In the summer of 1938, the marchioness was invited by Luis Bolin, Franco's chief of propaganda, to tour those areas of Spain held by the Nationalists and write an account of her findings.[14] The resulting report on her 2,500-mile journey appeared first in the USA, but extracts were subsequently reprinted in the *Western Mail*, a newspaper in which her husband had a controlling interest.[15] The editor of the leading newspaper in Wales, presumably under pressure from his proprietor, colluded in what was essentially a misrepresentation, although at other times both his paper and its sister the *South Wales Echo* maintained a stance of perplexed detachment from the Spanish war. At the time when Lady Bute was making her trip, her husband John was finalizing what was described at the time as 'the biggest real-estate sale ever to have taken place in Britain. For $32 million, he had concluded the sale of half the city of Cardiff. 20,000 houses were sold, 1,000 shops, 250 pubs, cinemas, whole suburbs.'[16]

Lady Bute was astounded by the absolute normality of what she saw on her journey through Franco's Spain: 'Touring foreigners evoked no surprise and were received with traditional Spanish courtesy.' Even though 'Red' trenches were only 4 kilometres away, conditions everywhere made it appear like peacetime. 'Spain wore her scars gracefully', wrote the marchioness. A vast amount of construction work was being undertaken. Roads were being repaired and tarred, houses and shops rebuilt. In Bilbao, five huge bridges, 'deliberately destroyed by defeated and vanquished Reds', had already been restored to use. Petrol was plentiful and available at every pump at normal prices. Food was abundant and of excellent quality with, her ladyship noted, 'the freshest fish being procurable even in central Spain'.

The marchioness was taken to Brunete, the scene of a terrible battle the previous summer. In July 1937, Republican forces had tried to take the western approaches of Madrid from Franco's Nationalists. Amongst them were 331 volunteers for the International Brigade. Alun Menai Williams from the Rhondda, who fought at Brunete, wrote that 'soldiers died from loss of blood with swollen tongues filling their parched mouths for want of water.' Only forty-two brigaders survived and most of those captured were mutilated before being killed.[17] Lady Bute lists only examples of Bolshevist cruelty: a church steeple used to house machine guns, young sisters taken prisoner and forced to march to Valencia, a hospital reduced to rubble. But, amongst the debris, the marchioness saw roses growing. Everywhere she finds the same optimistic spirit, that of a crusade to save Christianity not only for Spain but for the world. Lady Bute concludes her article with the Francoist rallying cry: '¡*Arriba España, Viva Franco*!'

Whether the observations of Augusta Crichton-Stuart were a conscious distortion of the situation in war-torn Spain or whether she was astonishingly gullible is debatable. What her article shows is that even in Wales the consensus in favour of Republican Spain had its limits. Apologists for the *Caudillo* were spreading the word that the war was almost over and that conditions in Spain were normal. The continued presence of refugees from yesterday's war was becoming incongruous.

It might be supposed that the refugees from Euskadi would have found a warm welcome among the ranks of the Welsh Nationalist party, but Plaid Genedlaethol Cymru remained resolutely indifferent to the children's predicament. Although officially neutral in its attitude to the Spanish Civil War, it is hard not to come to the conclusion that the party leadership considered a Nationalist victory to be the lesser of two evils. Of course, they felt uncomfortable with Franco's overt militarism and authoritarianism, but even more strongly they were conscious of the dangers of communism and suspicious of its influence over the Popular Front government. Moreover, the sober academics who made up the party hierarchy were willing to concede that some, at least, of the certainties that underpinned Nationalist Spain were valid. 'When Spain lifts its head again', wrote Ambrose Bebb, one of the co-founders of Plaid Cymru, 'we believe it will be a nation cleansed and purified by the present woes.'[18]

Bebb's political outlook had been greatly influenced by the 'blood and soil' nationalism of the French thinker, Charles Maurras. The party's president, Saunders Lewis, also had a strong attachment to continental culture, an attachment strengthened by his conversion to Catholicism in 1932. Aloof, disdainful, brilliant and compelling, Lewis sought to bring Wales back to what he called 'the European tradition', a journey others have described as a return to the Middle Ages. J. E. Daniel, who was to succeed Lewis as party president at the start of the Second World War, described the war in Spain as 'a symbol of the most important struggle of our time, that being the conflict between communism and the European tradition'.[19] In this context, involvement with the refugees might be seen as helping the innocent victims of war, but equally it could be seen as bringing comfort to one side, arguably the wrong side, in a cruel and chaotic struggle.

As early as July 1936, in *Y Ddraig Goch*, the official party journal, Bebb had cautioned against 'rushing like hotheads into a battle that is not ours to fight'. Nevertheless, at its conference the following month in Bala, the party did agree, amidst great acclamation, to send a message to President Aguirre expressing solidarity with the Basque people. But this was the high-water mark of the party's involvement with the Basque cause. While there were plenty in the rank and file of the party who had a left-wing perspective and saw no merit in Salazar or Franco, a chasm separated them from the party leadership.[20] Those, like Cyril Cule, who took an active role in helping Basque refugees as an expression of a commitment to Welsh internationalism were an aberration.

The failure of Welsh nationalism to support the Basque children may owe as much to inattentiveness as ideology. From the autumn of 1936 onwards, the attention of Plaid Genedlaethol Cymru was elsewhere. A week before Mola's army entered San Sebastian, three very respectable gentlemen committed their own illegal and seditious act. Writer and lecturer Saunders Lewis, schoolmaster D. J. Williams and Baptist minister Lewis Valentine stood in the dock of Caernarfon Court having, by their own admission, committed deliberate arson. 'The Three' had set fire to several empty buildings at Penyberth on the Llŷn peninsula causing thousands of pounds' worth of damage. The partly completed buildings were intended as a training camp and aerodrome for the RAF. For such a 'bombing school' to be built, Saunders Lewis wrote, 'one of the essential homes of Welsh culture, idiom and literature would have to be destroyed'. The farmhouse at Penyberth had been home to generations of Welsh poets and their patrons. The proposed structure was an outrage, an affront to the Welsh nation and a violation of a revered site. The insult was made more acute by the depraved purpose of the proposed building. Aerial bombing was described by the *Welsh Nationalist* newspaper as 'the official practice of murder . . . for the mangling of helpless bodies of little children, for the dropping of poison gas bombs on innocent and helpless people'.[21] The lawful path had been tried; over half a million signatures had been gathered in opposition; a meeting with the prime minister had been sought. In Northumberland and Dorset protests against similar proposals had been successful. In Llŷn, the project had been forced through in the teeth of overwhelming local hostility.

Penyberth was many things: a sincere expression of loathing of militarism, but also a calculated attempt to reignite Welsh nationalism as a political force, exactly four hundred years after Wales was incorporated into the union with England. Above all, it was a cry of pain at the desecration of a place that was a cradle of Welsh culture. At the first trial at Caernarfon, the jury had failed to reach a verdict. Heedless of the judge's warning not to use the court as a political platform, the Reverend Valentine had launched into speech that managed to be both apoplectic and apocalyptic:

> The English government's behaviour in the matter of the bombing school is exactly the behaviour of the new Anti-Christ throughout Europe. The establishment of a bombing school would make imminent the death of our Welsh nation . . . it is my responsibility to the Kingdom of God in Wales to strike this blow.[22]

At the retrial at the Old Bailey, 'The Three' were found guilty and sentenced to nine months' imprisonment in Wormwood Scrubs. A rally to celebrate their release was attended by a crowd of 15,000.

Penyberth was an intensely political act that quickly acquired iconic status. What it was not was an expression of international solidarity. In no sense did Plaid Cymru seek to link its opposition to militarism with support for the victims of fascism in the Basque country. Obvious parallels between Penyberth and the bombing of Guernica were not made. Struggles for autonomy in Catalonia and Euskadi seemingly had no relevance to the same struggle in Cymru. Plaid's energies, rhetoric and resources were diverted away from any meaningful engagement with the war in Spain by the bombing school campaign. It was *Tân yn Llŷn* (the fire in Llŷn) rather than events in a distant land that became their obsession.[23]

In Caerleon itself the children were met with a different kind of hostility; but this, too, was the product of indifference rather than outright hatred. The children had been in their new home less than a month when the town council decided to impose a rate on Cambria House. A 'mean act' according to one councillor and a sign, perhaps, that the children's welcome had not been quite as warm as it had appeared. The council's argument was that the home now had greater levels of occupancy. The proposed sum of £95 was reasonable, they argued, given that fifty-eight people now lived there. Councillor Jack Williams, a staunch champion of Cambria House throughout its existence, begged his colleagues to treat the children's case sympathetically and delay levying a rate. The payment of rates would place a crippling financial burden on the home which had running costs of £40 a week. After all, he argued, the children occupied only one-fifth of a very large building; the refugees had already spent £80 amongst local tradesmen; Caerleon orphanage paid a rate of only £8 a year and the town hall itself paid nothing in rates.[24]

The minutes of the meeting convey an undercurrent of antagonism and hurt. For Jack Williams, the debate was about more than filling the council coffers; it was about a betrayal of friendship. There is real passion in his appeal for the council to 'stay its hand' and not make life more difficult for the children. He was prepared, he said, to hold a ballot of the people of Caerleon and resign if the vote went against him. He demanded that the names of those voting be recorded and published in the newspapers. It was to no avail. The council decided by a margin of seven to three to impose a rate on the house. It was a petty and slightly spiteful episode, significant only as an indication that not everyone was prepared to go the extra mile on behalf of the exiled children.

11 DON'T SING THE SONGS OF THE PAST

THE DECEMBER 1938 EDITION of the *Cambria House Journal* had been dedicated to 'the great heroism of our soldiers, who are fighting unceasingly in the trenches, rain and snow, day and night, in horrible cold, in order to save our dear fatherland from the invaders'. The dream of turning back the Nationalist tide in Catalonia and achieving an epic victory for the Republic was still alive. No such illusion was possible by May. The wall newspaper on display in Cambria House showed government positions marked on a map by republican flags of red, yellow and mauve. It was a grim and graphic reminder of the scale of the rout. For the first time the young refugees had to come to terms with the bitter reality of defeat. An article about May Day, 'the feast of the workers . . . a great day. A day celebrated in Spain and throughout the world', ends on a melancholy note: 'We had hoped to return to a free country and set about the task of building up a new Spain, but this could not be. Still some day . . .'[1] From that point on, the question that had been raised ever since the fall of Bilbao, the previous June, was asked with even greater doggedness: now that their homeland is at peace, should not the children be returned there?

In 1938, Leo Abse, a 21-year-old law student, was despatched 'with the connivance of the Unions' to the Basque country to test the integrity of the requests from parents for the return of their children sheltering in Wales. With the help of an official in the

International Transport Federation, he was signed onto a cargo boat and slipped into Bilbao. The Republican cause was all but lost and the area was under heavy military occupation. It was a mission that was fraught with danger, but for Abse it was a poignant journey that he felt compelled to make. In July 1937, Leo Abse's closest friend, Sid Hamm, from Cardiff, had died fighting for the International Brigade in Brunete. It is very likely that Abse had himself considered joining the International Brigade, but the inexperienced recruit had been dissuaded by Arthur Horner, the 'tender Welsh Communist leader'. Hamm, more impetuous than his friend, had somehow 'slipped through the mesh'. Abse's clandestine visit confirmed the scepticism of those caring for the remaining refugees. He found that many of the appeals came from parents who had been coerced or were at risk from reprisals. Some of the letters had even been written from San Sebastian gaol.[2]

The children devote a lot of space in the *Journal* to trying to explain the complexity of the their predicament. An article in the May edition entitled 'Why I cannot return to Spain' tells the story of a father imprisoned for eighteen months under the previous rightist government for taking part in street demonstrations. Following his release he was accused of involvement in a bomb plot and sentenced to death. Only the Republican election victory saved him. By May 1939, the father was a refugee in France and his child was in Caerleon. If any member of that man's family were to return to Franco's Spain, argues the writer, it would mean persecution and probable death. In February 1939, over one four-day period 453,000 Spaniards crossed the border into France, a number without precedent. Many ended up in the brutal internment camps such as St Cyprien near the Pyrenees, camps that the photographer Robert Capa described as 'hell on sand'. Amongst the refugees on this terrible *Retirada* (retreat) were the parents of many of the children who remained in Wales.[3]

A letter, of questionable provenance, from Mrs T. S. of Monmouth asking why the children had not all been sent home, was printed in the May 1939 *Journal*. It provided the opportunity to explain once again that very few of the children had parents who were in a position to receive them: 'Most of their parents are in Franco's prisons or in French refugee camps. Five have no parents.'

Nevertheless, the steady trickle of repatriation continued. Some went home because they just could not face the prospect of another war. In June, it was agreed that seventeen children would be repatriated to Spain, with fifteen others being transferred to Cambria House in their place, from colonies in Scarborough and Liverpool. Some of these newcomers came from homes where behaviour was 'not so good'. The remarkable Mrs Fernandez described how she dealt with the problem: 'Cambria House was one of the best. In other homes they just did not understand each other and they had behaved atrociously. I called them together and warned them. They were expected to behave and they behaved.'[4]

One of the boys spoke of his sadness at leaving behind those who, for over two years, had become his brothers and sisters. He also spoke of the mood of comradeship and happiness he had found at Cambria House and especially the support that had come from the miners of south Wales. Another, who was remaining in Wales, wrote of his mixed emotions: envy that his friends were seeing their parents, but horror that they were returning to a country governed by Franco. 'We thought', he said, 'that we should all go back together to a free Spain.'[5]

That last summer, some of the children spent a fortnight in Aberavon giving fund-raising concerts on the beach. Every day while they sang on the sands, the children could see, just off the coast, aeroplanes practising for war. As the bombs dropped over their targets, sending up clouds of smoke and spray, youthful minds raced back to the terrifying events in their homeland. Images of annihilation returned – aircraft flying low across fields in Spain, bombs falling and scattering pieces of flying shrapnel. For two years comradeship and mutual support had kept such horrors at bay, but as the August holidays came to a close, war finally caught up with the children of Cambria House.

Refugees from war have a terrible expertise in survival. Articles in the *Journal* in the autumn months of 1939 bear witness to gentle minds reliving scouring experiences, juveniles with a sad proficiency in enduring warfare. In the November 1939 issue of the magazine, 'A Spanish Friend' mourns the loss of innocence which experience of totalitarian warfare has inflicted on a rising generation: 'Children, in spite of their tender age, describe, with no fear of being mistaken, how trenches should be constructed, what would be the best kind of shelter in case of an aerial bombardment and a number of other things that they ought to know nothing about.'[6]

The pages of the *Journal* also provided an outlet for expressions of anger against those who had remained indifferent to the looming menace of fascism and unmoved by the distress of its victims. Both Cyril Cule and Jack Williams wrote highly political pieces. In tones of measured fury Williams argued that the children at Caerleon were the offspring of those who had fought to stem the tide of fascism. For three long years, he said, the defenders of the Spanish Republic had told anyone prepared to listen that they were fighting on behalf of all humanity. They suffered and were still suffering. Fascism could have been broken, he argued, and a European conflagration avoided if they had been supported in their struggle. Cule added in his article that the heroic men and women who fought for the Republic were now entitled to turn to the rest of Europe and say, 'I told you so'.

In September 1939, Britain finally entered the war against fascism. As a direct consequence, many of the refugees in Caerleon would be returned to Franco's Spain and the place that had been their home for over two years would be closed. This was a bitter irony that was not lost on anyone at Cambria House.[7] There was one further irony. The reason why the children and staff were compelled to vacate their home was that Cambria House had been requisitioned by the army. The children's new residence, Vale View, was a house built to accommodate twenty people. As the colony consisted of sixty, including staff, an appeal was made for private homes to take in some of the children. Homes were found for eighteen of them. Then, after the children had spent only a fortnight in their new home, the military claimed the use of Vale View. Once again, the colony was moved, this time to 18 Cross Street, a house with even more limited accommodation. A further eight children were placed in various private homes leaving thirty-five children and adults living in very crowded circumstances.

The agonizing decision was taken at the end of November to return a further twenty-five boys and girls to their parents in Spain. Each would be returning to severe food shortages and political repression, but these deprivations were outweighed by the need to reunite families and avoid the uncertainties of life in a country that was itself at war. It was, recalled Mrs Fernandez, like a family splitting up again.[8]

By the end of 1938, 1,300 of the refugee children who had arrived in Southampton had been returned to Spain, and a further 230 were awaiting investigation. Those who went back soon learned not to speak of the days of hope, not to sing the songs of the past. They had returned to what one writer has called a 'vengeful, half starving Spain'.[9] For many, it was a deeply unpleasant experience. The children were demonized as 'miniature monsters'. Their exile was either the result of 'moral delinquency' or they had been 'morally abandoned'. They were not only misguided but wicked. In an interview, Franco made his views clear about these children of the Reds. 'It is not possible', he said, 'without taking precautions, to return to society or to social circulation harmful, perverted, politically and morally poisoned elements.'[10]

The intervention of a world war meant that it was not until the late 1940s that any of the Welsh exiles were able to visit their homeland. These were hungry years and when Josefina went back in 1948, she was appalled by the food shortages. On her first visit to Bilbao after the war, Maria Fernandez found that people were afraid to talk. Those young refugees who had gone back had, she said, been 'herded into convents and really brainwashed'. At the end of 1940, there were still officially 240,916 prisoners in concentration camps, 7,762 of whom had been sentenced to death.[11]

Pro-Franco lobbyists were not blind to the propaganda value of accounts of repatriation. As correspondent for the *Catholic Herald*, the Australian writer, Paul McGuire travelled with 130 children from Southampton through 'Red France' and records their jubilant arrival in 'peaceful, industrious and Catholic Spain', where he found 'the cry of Christ the King on everyone's lips'.[12]

Even those who were relatively well disposed towards the new regime found that they were treated with suspicion on their homecoming. A former teacher from Sketty Park, Maria Luisa Fuentes wrote about her return in April 1938:

> In the train we were almost all refugees. We went across the whole of France, changed trains once and arrived in Hendaye. We crossed the border on foot and we found ourselves in the Spanish customs faced with questions.

> 'Do you have English money? Do you work for the Reds?' In Irun, we had expected to feel at home but after one month I was called in by the police. In the station, they continued with the interrogation. 'Why did you work there?' I replied without wavering: 'Because I am young and I did not want to be killed in a bombing raid.'[13]

There remained in south Wales some thirty-two children who could not safely be returned because their parents were dead, had disappeared into fascist prison camps or were themselves refugees. In some cases, desperate letters had been received from parents describing the terrible deprivations and dangers in Spain and appealing for their loved ones to remain in Britain.

The financial needs of the South Wales Basque Children's Committee were not as great as they had been, but income to support the remaining children had fallen alarmingly. The committee asked for help to avoid a catastrophe. In September, there had been a sudden drop in circulation of the *Journal*. Fund-raising concerts and football games became impossible because of the blackout. Jack Williams appealed to the friends and supporters not to forget the children – 'Victims of Fascist aggression who still need our help.'[14]

The National Joint Committee reported that, by November 1941, the great majority of Basque refugees had returned to Spain. Only 416 of the 4,000 children who had arrived on board the *Habana* were still in Britain and those who remained had either been adopted or taken in by concerned families until the uncertainties of war faded. Cross Street in Caerleon was the only settlement in Wales to avoid closure. Its continuing existence was assured by an annual grant from the South Wales Miners' Federation.[15] By then it was home to ten young people, a dwindling band engaged for the most part in various training schemes relating to horticulture or mechanics. It was not until 1947 that the colony finally closed its doors when the very last of the refugees flew the nest to begin new lives in Argentina and Chile.[16]

In an article entitled 'War – and now what shall we do?', Cyril Cule attempted to sum up the essential spirit of Cambria House, a place born out of suffering, but grounded in a firm resolve that out of chaos a better world would emerge. 'Nothing in this world can possibly kill this spirit', he wrote. 'In many ways, these children are older than their years . . . They have simply learnt the lessons of their own experience and such lessons will make them very useful to whatever community they may belong to. They are not a burden but an asset.'[17]

12 NOT OURS, BUT OURS TO LOOK AFTER

ALVARO DID NOT WANT to go back home but he had no choice. It was 1939 and another war menaced Europe, so he was hastily repatriated. He arrived back in Spain to find his brother, a former soldier in the Republican Army, in a concentration camp. His father and mother had gone back to San Sebastian. They were not running anymore. The elation and the despair of his return remain with Alvaro:

> It was marvellous, you know, just to see your mother when you have missed her, we embraced we cried. But the poverty, it was horrendous, it was absolutely poor. Our suffering was dreadful because in my family only my father and me were working, just the two of us. And I was only a small, little kid getting seven pesetas a week.

During the Second World War he continued to make unsuccessful attempts to leave Spain. He never lost his belief that, if he could get back to Wales, he would be welcomed with open arms He and his friend Pedro even tried to enlist in the British army:

> The two of us just went to the British Embassy and told the man we wanted to fight in the war. And he said to us we had to go to Gibraltar to join up. Well, good God,

> how can we manage to get from San Sebastian to Gibraltar? Oh, it was most disappointing.

On another occasion, the two friends managed to get aboard a British cargo boat bound for Cardiff. Neither of them had a passport or papers:

> We wanted to escape you see – we knew we had friends in Wales and all that. We met some sailors in a bar and asked about being taken on that boat. We thought 'this is it, we are going to Cardiff now!' But they asked us for money and we didn't have any money, so they chucked us out. Oh, it was cruel. I remember early, early in the morning the sailors said, 'Out you go'.

For Alvaro, the years of separation from Wales came to an end on 13 December 1947. L. D. Owen-Edwards of Trefelin, who had befriended Alvaro during his time in the Brechfa camp, agreed to sponsor his application to enter Britain. Alvaro remembers: 'We kept in touch all the years, years and years and they came for a holiday at San Sebastian. That was after the war. And we talked about it and they said, "Would you like to come back to Carmarthen?"' He did not hesitate for one moment. The application was made. Such immigration visas were only granted in rare circumstances, but for once the Home Office showed some humanity. Alvaro was granted a one-month visa on the condition that he lived with his host family. The one month stretched to three months, then to a year. There was a problem though. The early visas specified that under no circumstances should he work. He had served his apprenticeship in Spain as a precision engineer, but to fill the hours in Carmarthen he swept the floor in a local garage. His daily routine had been monitored and he was called to the Labour Exchange to explain why he had infringed his conditions of residency. For several months, the fear of being sent back to Spain hung over him. Then, finally, an indefinite right to stay was granted, provided that he notified the police if he changed address.

When he came back to Carmarthen, Alvaro spoke no English; at the camps there had been no schools and little need to speak anything other than Spanish. Now, he was the only Spaniard for miles around and as such slightly exotic. He would have to make his own way. But he was young and he had survived warfare, surmounted hardship and exile. He did not expect things to be easy. He eventually found a job as a welder and panel beater. One of his early commissions was to make a huge metal top hat to be suspended outside a shop in Lammas Street. It hangs there to this day. He also revealed a talent for football, playing over many seasons for Carmarthen Town. He married a local girl, started a family and lived in the same comfortable house in Carmarthen for forty years. He had the friendship and respect of neighbours whom he had known for a generation. He was satisfied at how his life had turned out: 'I haven't got any regrets anyway. I live an honest life. I am happy. I always had a job, so that's all there is to it. I can go anywhere in this town and find a friend.'[1]

Josefina and Gerardo could not return to Bilbao. There was no one to go back to anymore. As the rebel armies advanced on Bilbao their mother had escaped, put on a ship for Catalonia by their father. He had stayed behind, moving with the Basque government to Santander and the children had lost contact with him. Later, they discovered that he had been caught by the Nationalists, tried, imprisoned and shot, allegedly while trying to escape. He was politically active and could expect no mercy. On the day Santander fell, there were no classes in Cambria House. Cule wrote: 'the children were too grief stricken to think of anything but the plight of their parents and elders'.[2]

A teacher from Newport, Miss Ward, recognizing great potential, took Josefina under her wing. Josefina had absolutely no English when she arrived, she and her teacher had to communicate in pidgin French, but she learned very quickly. Miss Ward invited the youngster to her home to have extra lessons and spurred on her learning with the promise of a day out in London. It worked. 'She did take me to London for the day', says Josefina, 'and I think we saw everything.' Christopher Hill had a friend who was one of the teachers at the much admired Badminton School, in Bristol, a school that numbered Iris Murdoch and Indira Gandhi amongst its alumni. He and Miss Ward encouraged Josefina to apply and in September 1938 she won a place as a boarder. She still remembers the essay she wrote to secure her scholarship: 'It was about the

Spanish countryside in summer, where people have to work from dawn to dusk and had to have a siesta because of the heat.'[3]

Badminton had a broad and progressive curriculum. Its charismatic headmistress, Miss Beatrice May Baker, had a deep personal influence on her pupils. The girls were encouraged to be aware of world affairs and internationalism. She insisted on the right to freedom of expression and promoted a questioning approach to learning. 'In chapel', wrote Miss Baker, 'Jesus often had to share the stage with Lenin.'[4] In this tolerant atmosphere Josefina thrived. At the time, she wrote, 'There is much discipline, but at the same time there is liberty'. She remembers a course called 'Progress of Civilisation', learning history through peaceful developments rather than conflicts, and 'news of the day', a lesson studying that morning's newspapers.[5] A refugee from Nazi Germany became Josefina's best friend. She was one of about a dozen girls at Badminton who were given sanctuary from Europe's many conflicts, 'suffering because of the egotism of some selfish men', as Josefina wrote in 1939. At Badminton Josefina learnt that it was possible for different nationalities to live together in harmony. She has remained convinced of that possibility ever since.

Josefina's first weeks in her new school were overshadowed by *La Retirada* (the retreat). In February 1939, Barcelona, where Josefina's mother was sheltering, fell to Franco and her mother, along with almost half a million other 'foreign undesirables', fled across the border to the hellish refugee camps of southern France. Josefina was understandably distraught and only the kindness of her new companions got her through those wretched days. Remarkably, Christopher Hill did manage to secure a passage for her mother to come to Wales but the move was not a success and at the end of the Second World War she returned home.

In the *Cambria House Journal* of August 1939, one of the staff at Caerleon wrote in praise of the 'remarkable scholastic success of 'JA': 'She is a credit to the colony. She speaks and writes perfect English and her teachers have sent us very favourable reports.'[6] The writer predicts that she will go on to study history or literature. She was still at Badminton when the Second World War broke out, taking her School Certificate exams in between visits to the air-raid shelter. The British Council offered Josefina a scholarship to study English at Birmingham University, but as an alien she required authorization to travel. The local police superintendent personally delivered the necessary permit to Josefina on the platform at Risca station. As Josefina says, 'You don't forget things like that'.

Most of the young refugees who arrived in Wales experienced nothing but kindness and there is still a feeling of intense gratitude to countless ordinary people for the welcome they gave. 'We were invited all over the place'; 'We were welcomed with great kindness'; 'I will never forget Welsh hospitality'. Sometimes, it is the relatively small acts of kindness that stick in the memory: the tickets to the cinema or trips to the seaside, gifts of sweets or small toys. Charlie Jones of Water Street in Carmarthen who bought José a suitcase, Vernon Mason of Six Bells in Abertillery and Eleanor and Julian Estanez, a Welsh-Spanish couple from Dowlais who opened their homes to Gerardo. Once a fortnight, on a Sunday, George Phillips would ask twelve Basque children to come for tea at his parents' house at 32 Corelli Street in Newport. On alternate Sundays, his best friend Jack Hart would do the same at his house. George's parents William and Ethel already had eight children of their own to feed and making ends meet was a struggle, but they were willing to share what little they had. Such acts of inconspicuous kindness deserve to be remembered.[7]

Mari Carmen, a refugee from the Margate colony, was adopted and loved by the Jones family from Barry. One war ended in 1939 and another broke out and still Mari Carmen had heard nothing from her parents. Margate, situated on the south coast, was dangerously exposed to a German invasion. So when Bessie, a worker at the colony, invited Mari Carmen to go back with her to her home town in south Wales she jumped at the chance. She found herself part of a strong and loving family. As well as Bessie and her two brothers, there was a profoundly deaf sister, Mary Jones. It was Mary who became her foster mother. 'Dad' Jones, who worked in an office in Barry docks, was in the Home Guard and kept an allotment. Thirteen-year-old Maria, as Mari Carmen became known, flourished. She did well at school and began to speak good English, with a lilting Welsh accent. She got a job in nursing and for a while helped in the Basque colony at Carshalton. When 'Mam' Jones went into hospital, Maria returned to Barry to keep the household together. Finally, in 1946, Maria's parents managed to trace her. She no longer felt abandoned but her roots were now in Wales.[8]

Not all were so content. For Paula, already distressed by the fighting in Bilbao, the evacuation had been particularly harrowing. Being uprooted was almost more than her young mind could bear and even the company of her two sisters, Angelita and Rosita, did little to provide solace. At Cambria House she did gradually regain her spirits. For an interlude she was happy, but when the colony moved to a smaller house, the three sisters were split up. Paula was taken in by the Burton family who were active in the Spanish Committee in Neath. Those years were a 'horrible experience', says Paula. Separated from her sisters, she was terribly lonely. School was incomprehensible: 'sums, I could cope with, nothing much else'. At the age of fourteen she began work in a canteen despite not speaking much English. She met her husband at a dance and, at twenty, she was married. She says her life started at that moment.[9]

There is no doubt that a sense of having been abandoned affected many of the children greatly. Cyril Cule wrote that at first discipline in Caerleon was extremely difficult as the children were in a confused state of mind and their nerves were on edge. They were continually having nightmares and were worried about the fate of their parents. The pictures they drew were invariably of aeroplanes dropping bombs on an ambulance. The ambulances would be clearly marked with a red cross, the aeroplane with a swastika. In the camps, they had known intense loneliness, though they were seldom alone. Robbed of a proper childhood, their higgledy-piggledy lives were often weighed down by low spirits and melancholy.[10]

Many of the *niños* still passionately defend the achievements of the Republican government in the few years before it was snuffed out by Franco. Experiences during those turbulent years have given them sympathy for the underdog which time has not eroded. They continue to identify with the uprooted and the dispossessed. A passion for social justice was shaped by the convulsions in Spain. Cyril Cule wrote: 'never before or since have I ever found people so politically conscious at such an early age'. He recalled a conversation with a 14-year-old refugee at the time when Franco's forces were advancing on Santander. The girl can only have been Josefina. 'What are people thinking of in this country?' she asked, angrily. 'Another Abyssinia? After Spain, it will be France and then England. Don't they know that?' 'Yes, we know that very well', replied Cule, 'but it's unfortunate that we have this government.' 'Government?' she retorted, 'but what are the workers doing?'[11]

In the course of a long life, Cyril Cule went on to teach in Armenia and the Lebanon. He wrote two books in Welsh as well as many pamphlets. His obituary in 2002 noted that he felt a tremendous empathy with the Armenians and the Basques and that he loved Cuban culture. He subscribed to three publications: *Beecraft* magazine, the Welsh Baptist paper *Seren* and the *Morning Star*.[12]

At Cambria House, the children had been taught to recognize that whatever wrongs were being inflicted on the Basque people, they were not unique in their suffering. Lessons were devoted to Italy's invasion of Abyssinia and the Japanese attack on China. When the persecution of the Jews grew ever more intense and brutal, Mrs Fernandez suggested that the children send a letter of sympathy to the chief rabbi in Cardiff. In reply, the synagogue made a donation of £50 to Cambria House.

In Colwyn Bay, in December 1938, only a few months after the last of the Basque children had left, a public meeting was held. Its purpose was to lobby the Home Office on behalf of a new wave of persecuted people, the Jews seeking to leave Hitler's Germany. The individuals and organizations who were active in this new campaign were the same people who had worked tirelessly on behalf of the Basques. Once again they asked for 'active sympathy' and for contributions. Once again they were met with the argument that unemployment was serious enough in this country without the added burden of refugees. Once again the authorities insisted that they would make no contribution to expenses in connection with the refugees and all costs must be borne by voluntary institutions. Once again the authorities delayed and obstructed applications.[13]

Overwhelmingly, those children who remained in this country went on to have contented and successful lives. The *niños* brought nothing to their new country but energy, courage and a level-headed attitude. The convulsions in Spain had stolen much of their childhood but there is remarkably little self-pity or bitterness. Time and distance have not lessened the love they feel for the land of their birth, but home is here.

For many years, the Felipe sisters, who were by then Mrs Hanford and Mrs Griffiths, ran a wool shop in Skewen. Paula and her husband still live in the town, at the centre of a large, supportive family. Josefina met her future husband at a French circle at Birmingham University. When he returned from the war they were married and settled in south Wales where she found a job teaching Spanish. They still live in the south Wales valleys, not too far from Caerleon. Her brother, Gerardo, one of the youngest refugees to leave Bilbao, spent the early years of the war 'semi-fostered' in Galen Uchaf. He attended the primary school in Caerleon and later went on to Abersychan Grammar School. He now divides his year between a home on the Welsh borders and his house in Australia. José Armolea, who at the age of eleven came to Brechfa with his brother Martín, left Margate colony to lodge with a friend in Barnet. A succession of factory jobs led to a career as a manager with Smiths Industries. On his retirement, he was awarded the British Empire Medal for services to industry.[14] Juanito Benamete, the brother of an anarchist, became a celebrated pastry cook and made the cake for the investiture of the prince of Wales.

There are poignant tales, too. One of the Caerleon boys found his way into the British army at the start of the Second World War and was killed at Dunkirk. Alberto Rodrigues, who was taken in by a family in Neath, found that his father, who had been a city official in Bilbao, had been executed by Falangist soldiers. He emigrated to Mexico with his mother and sister. Many of the children had no choice but to return home to Spain. Among these was the talented artist Eusebio Asencor, a student at Newport College who was last heard of living in Bilbao. Another was 10-year-old Isabel Barrientos. She had been unofficially adopted by a couple called Trevor and Iris Berry. Long afterwards, she wrote: 'They loved me as if I'd been their daughter . . . They humoured all my whims and, as I didn't care for tea, Iris brought my breakfast up to me in bed: orange juice and cocoa with biscuits.' But the idyll could not last. The Civil War ended and Isabel's mother made contact and asked for her to be sent back home. The Berrys, desperate not to be separated from Isabel, tried to arrange for her mother to be brought over to this country but, in 1939, such a plan was unworkable. Isabel returned home on her eleventh birthday to wretched poverty. She remembers seeing dogs abandoned on the streets dying of hunger. The Spanish Civil War had not long ended and there was no work. Isabel, who still lives in Bilbao, has fond memories of her Welsh family:

> Mr and Mrs Berry wrote many letters to me sending lots of kisses. They remembered me constantly. I too used to reply, but I don't remember how we stopped writing to each other. They were very difficult times. But I never forget them and I continue to remember them with great affection. I still keep some photographs of them and of the *colonia*.[15]

Esperanza Careaga was another of the estimated thirty-five refugees who made their homes in Wales. Her story is particularly moving. She left Bilbao on 26 April 1937, eight days before her sixth birthday. At the quayside in Bilbao officials unexpectedly separated Espe from her brother Alberto. She sailed on the *Habana* to Southampton and from there travelled to Colchester and Margate before ending up in Cambria House. Alberto was evacuated to Russia and it was to be fifty years before they would see each other again. There was no possibility of Espe's returning to Spain at the end of the Civil War. Their father, a prisoner in one of Franco's camps, had vanished forever; their mother was unwell and destitute. In December 1939, just two days before Christmas, Esperanza was given a home with George and Gertrude Harris in Barry. She remained there until she married in 1958.[16]

In all the years she has spent in south Wales, Paula can only recall one example of racial antagonism and that single instance she turned to her advantage:

> People in the village accepted us. Most people were curious more than anything. I think I had more backchat when I came to Neath about being a foreigner. When I walked into a dance, someone said, 'Oh, a Spanish onion'. Someone told me to say: 'a Welsh leek smells just as bad'. Well I was very proud of that.[17]

Josefina tells a story of a similar example of juvenile malice that now provokes laughter rather than anger:

> There was a little boy who often stood outside the gate. As we went by, he would mumble 'sangre tonto'. For years I wondered what he meant. Then suddenly it came to me. He had gone to a dictionary and looked up the exact translation of 'bloody fool'![18]

There are many heroes in this story, but supreme amongst them is Maria Fernandez. The years she spent caring for the Basque children were the most vital of her long life. Long after she retired, she explained her reasons for becoming involved with the Basque children: 'Why did I do it? It is simple: I believed in the Spanish Republic and I have always loved people.'[19] Until her death in 2001, at the age of ninety-seven, she kept in touch with almost all of 'her children', many scattered across south Wales, others in exile in France, Chile or Argentina. To the end of her days she remained fiercely proud of what they had achieved together:

> They thought the world of them in the local community. When the children were on holiday in Port Talbot, the manager of Woolworths gave them all a little present; so you can see what sort of children they were. I was very lucky to land them. It was a great era.[20]

She also had justifiable pride of her achievement in making Cambria House one of the most successful colonies in the country and at every opportunity expressed her gratitude for the support it received from the ordinary people of south Wales of whatever political persuasion. 'Labour, Liberal, Communist, Conservative, we had a bit of everything . . . It's amazing how we ambled along. Up and down the valleys, everywhere we were received with open arms.' The deepest praise she reserves for the south Wales miners and the welcome they gave to foreign children seeking asylum in a foreign land:

> There was a deep, deep feeling from them. Without the miners, a lot would have had to have gone back. From

> Will Paynter and Tom Jones there was never a refusal of any kind. Whenever we had no money, they never refused us anything. Wonderful people.[21]

A press release put out at the end of the summer of 1938 encapsulates the wonderful capacity for human kindness and solidarity that underpins the whole story of the Basque refugees in Wales. Folk who had so shamefully little themselves willingly shared their precious time and possessions; never losing sight of the fact that, however unfairly, they had been treated, there were others who had been dealt an even harsher blow. The National Joint Committee (NJC) bulletin recorded this act of humanity:

> Fifty three children spent a week's holiday during August 1938 with miners' families at Abertillery, Six Bells, Dowlais, Cwmbran and Blaenavon. Behind this bare announcement lies a fine story of human solidarity. The Welsh miners, out of very small salaries, are already contributing generously to Spanish Relief through their Federation. This year for the first time in their lives many of them were granted a week's holiday with pay. They could not afford to go away themselves so instead they decided to ask the Basque Children's Committee to let each family have one Basque child as a guest for a week. In this way the Basque children had seven days' happiness in a home atmosphere, playing with miners' children and generally enjoying themselves to the top of their bent.[22]

Such generosity, of spirit as well as of purse, could surely not have been bettered. The kind of society that can produce such decency and solidarity is exceptional. A communal response was fashioned by conditions in Wales in that most radical of decades. It was so intense because, not in spite of, its happening in the depths of a terrible economic depression. Through the presence of these children profound political realities were brought *directly home* to ordinary families. It was a partisan response. There was little room anywhere in Wales for ambivalence, no real appetite to weigh the relative merits of competing causes or parties. It was a response that was part of a long history of rallying to the cause of the downtrodden, a tradition of dissent and radicalism going back beyond Chartism and stretching forward to the miners' strike of our own era.

The young refugees who arrived here on board the *Habana* were met by government and press with a jumble of emotions, compassion, indifference and even, occasionally, spite. They had been driven into exile by premeditated military terror and many returned to Spain to suffer years of political repression. In the years since 1937, countless other peoples have undergone the same experiences as the young Basques and how we have responded to their plight tells us much about our society. A cursory glance at today's media will tell you that our own age does not lack for meanness of spirit. Perhaps an earlier age illuminates our own.

The workings of fate meant that a few hundred young people fleeing a hideous conflict found a home in Wales, most for a few years, some for a lifetime. It should be a matter of pride that in the hardest of times, the obligation towards those children was discharged with such humanity. The shared values that underpinned the popular response deserve celebration, particularly at a time when such values are themselves in danger of slipping into history. If there are defining moments in our collective past, episodes that reveal the particular pattern of a people or society, then let the fellow feeling shown towards young exiles from a foreign land be recorded as one such moment.

NOTES

1 AN UNCERTAIN WELCOME

1 *Daily Mail*, 15 July 1937; *Time Magazine*, 26 July 1937.

2 *Western Mail*, 30 August 1937.

3 *North Wales Weekly News*, 11 August 1937.

4 *North Wales Pioneer*, 22 July 1937.

5 *Welshman* (Carmarthen), 23 July 1937.

6 The foreign secretary was lionized by sections of the press. A gushing report of a meeting in the *North Wales Weekly News* stated that 'His sincerity is obvious. His firmness no less firm because of his suavity.' To this might be added a comment from G. T. Garratt: 'To a generation of Spaniards our foreign minister will be remembered as *el gancho*, the dandy, who lured his country from its duty with soft words.' (G. T. Garratt, *Mussolini's Roman Empire* (Harmondsworth: Penguin, 1937), p. 213.

7 Speech to the House of Commons, 28 October 1937, *Hansard*, vol. 328, cc 232–3.

8 Garratt, *Mussolini's Roman Empire*, p. 243. Garratt was honorary administrator for the National Joint Committee for Spanish Relief and had spent most of 1937 in eastern Spain. Before that he was the *Guardian* correspondent in Abyssinia.

9 *Daily Mail*, 14 July 1937. The paper's editorial outlined three guiding principles of foreign policy: 'Rearm at top speed, keep out of all trouble that does not concern us and get on good terms with Germany and Italy.'

10 Garratt, *Mussolini's Roman Empire*, p. 173. The book is essentially about the ambitions of Mussolini, although chapters 11 to 14 deal with the situation in Spain.

11 In his diaries Harold Nicholson wrote of Baldwin: 'No man has ever left office in such a blaze of affection.' *Diaries and Letters* (London: Faber, 1968), p. 113

12 W. Paynter, Forward to Hywel Francis, *Miners against Fascism: Wales and the Spanish Civil War* (London: Lawrence and Wishart, 1984).

13 Maitland had been imprisoned as a conscientious objector during the First World War. Elected as a Member of Parliament for the University of Wales in 1923 he lost his seat the following year. A minister of religion, he served as chairman of the Peace Pledge Union for three years after the Second World War. He took his own life in 1949.

14 The only significant exception to the Aliens Act of 1905 was the influx of Belgium refugees who arrived here having fled the advancing German armies in 1914.

15 Talk given by Dr Tom Buchanan to Basque Children of '37 Association UK (3 October 2009).

16 *National Joint Committee Bulletin*, autumn 1937, reported that the public 'no longer felt the same sense of urgency that had gripped the country at the end of April'.

2 BROTHERS OF THE BLOOD

1 However, the widely accepted view of the Basques as Europe's aboriginals was given a jolt in 2001 when a study by British and American scientists discovered considerable genetic similarities between the Basques and the Celts of Ireland and Wales.

2 *Caernarvon and Denbigh Herald*, 23 April 1937, and *Time magazine*, 3 May 1937. In fact General Foch, born in Tarbes, was the son of a civil servant from Provence.

3 Gwyn Jones, *Welsh Review*, 1, 3 (April 1939).

4 *Western Mail*, 6 May 1937.

5 *Western Mail*, 26 May 1937.

6 In Hywel Francis, *Miners Against Fascism: Wales and the Spanish Civil War* (London: Lawrence and Wishart, 1984), p. 126.

7 'Spain everybody's war', *Time Magazine*, 12 April 1937.

8 Mark Kurlansky, *The Basque History of the World* (London: Vintage, 2000), p. 18.

9 John Hooper, *The New Spaniards* (London: Penguin, 2006) has an excellent chapter on Basque history and identity.

10 Kurlansky, *The Basque History of the World*, p. 3.

11 Dorothy Thompson, 'On the record', *New York Herald Tribune*, 30 April 1937.

12 George Steer, *The Tree of Gernika* (London: Hodder and Stoughton, 1938; reprinted London: Faber, 2009), p. 398.

13 Albert F. Calvert, *Impressions of Spain* (London: Phillip and Son, 1903).

14 A list of children in Cambria House drawn up for 'adoption' comments that Eufemia and Juan-Mari 'speak Basque fluently, as well as the more usual Castilian'.

15 Most of the surviving 'children' interviewed for this book were not ethnic Basques and none could speak Basque fluently, yet all, to varying degrees, expressed pride in the achievements of the short-lived Basque Republic and a sense of identity with Euskadi.

16 G. A. Williams, 'Imperial south Wales' in *The Welsh in their History* (London: Croom Helm, 1982), p. 184.

17 Mike Thomas, 'Not unlike Bilbao', *Planet*, 192 (December/January 2008/2009), 68–74. From 1888 onwards the Dowlais Iron and Steel Company gradually shifted its production to East Moors in Cardiff. Proximity to the docks cut transport costs for imports of Basque ore and exports of Welsh steel.

18 Maria Fernandez (1987), SCC AUD/439.

19 Ibid.

20 On the issue of whether or not the Spanish community in Dowlais was unanimous in its support for the Republic there is some debate. Hywel Francis asserts in *Miners Against Fascism* that 'sympathy for the Spanish Republic and its Popular Front Government among these Spanish families was, as we have seen, total and unequivocal' (p. 203).

21 Abercraf Community Study (1972). SWCC / AUD 2000. Interview with Casimira Duenos (née Esteban). As an example of the degree of integration in the community, Hywel Francis cites Gregorio Esteban, born in Baracaldo, who taught Spanish through the medium of Welsh in the miners welfare hall in Abercraf.

22 SWML, Onllwyn Spanish Aid Committee minutes, 7 March 1937, cited in Francis, *Miners Against Fascism*, p. 205.

23 The relationship between the Asturias and Welsh miners is the subject of an article by Rob Stradling, 'A fine romance', *Planet*, 196, 77–83. It is also dealt

with by H. Francis and D. Smith, *The Fed: A History of South Wales Miners in the Twentieth Century* (London: Lawrence & Wishart, 1980).

24 N. M. C. Sinclair, *The Tiger Bay Story* (Cardiff: Butetown History and Arts Project, 1993), chapter 4.

25 R. Stradling, *Cardiff and the Spanish Civil War* (Cardiff: University of Wales Press, 1996), p. 49.

26 The contribution made by the Spanish communities of Dowlais and Abercraf to the International Brigade is admirably documented by Hywel Francis in *Miners Against Fascism.*

27 Almost all the children in south Wales spent time with the communities at Abercraf and Dowlais. In an interview in 2008 Gerardo Álvarez recalled with great affection the Estabanez family of Dowlais who 'semi-fostered' him between 1939 and 1941.

28 *Daily Mail*, 1 July 1937, a report on the taking of the important iron-ore-exporting port of Castro Urdiales.

29 In interviews, several of the surviving refugees remember being pleased to be going to Wales or recall being told that they were lucky to be sent there. 'Of course', says José Armolea, 'we knew there were a lot of left-wing associations between Bilbao and south Wales'.

3 A BADGE OF HONOUR

1 See, for example, K. O. Morgan, 'Socialists and Radicals responding as men had done in 1789 to the cause of repressed liberty overseas. In this case in the face of insurgency and increasingly well armed Fascism'. *Rebirth of a Nation: A History of Modern Wales* (Oxford: Oxford University Press, 1981), p. 290.

2 G . A. Williams, *When was Wales? A History of the Welsh* (Harmondsworth: Penguin, 1985), pp. 270–1.

3 R. Stradling, *Wales and the Spanish Civil War: The Dragon's Dearest Cause?* (Cardiff: University of Wales Press, 2004), p. 6.

4 H. Francis, *Miners Against Fascism* (London: Lawrence and Wishart, 1984), p. 80.

5 These figures are quoted by the South Wales International Brigade Memorial Trust Committee. In his book Professor Stradling lists 153 volunteers who gave home addresses in Wales.

6 W. Paynter, *My Generation* (London: Allen and Unwin), pp. 61–2.

7 A discussion of whether the relationship between Spain and Wales really had a 'special quality' at the time of the Civil War is at the heart of Rob Stradling's book, *Wales and the Spanish Civil War.*

8 D. G. Evans, *A History of Wales 1906–2000* (Cardiff: University of Wales Press, 2000), p. 95.

9 An outstanding, detailed account of the struggle in the mining communities is H. Francis and D. Smith, *The Fed: A History of the South Wales Miners in the Twentieth Century* (London: Lawrence and Wishart, 1980).

10 From Auden's poem 'September 1939'.

11 J. Morris, *The Matter of Wales: Epic Views of a Small Country* (Harmondsworth: Penguin, 1984), p. 410. Francis and Smith identify the volunteer as Will Lloyd of Aberdare. *The Fed*, p. 354.

12 Lewis Jones, *We Live: The Story of a Welsh Mining Valley* ([1937] London: Lawrence and Wishart, 1978).

13 I. Jenkins, *Idris Davies of Rhymney – A Personal Memoir* (Llandysul: Gwasg Gomer, 1986).

14 The quotation forms the title of a study carried out by Lewis Mates into the activities of the Communist Party in the north-east, 'A most fruitful period? The north-east and the Popular Front period, 1935–39', *North East History*, 36 (2004), 54–98.

15 Michael Foot, in the first volume of his book on Bevan, describes the ban on appearing on platforms with communists as a 'technicality'. On numerous occasions Bevan participated in 'Unity' campaigns. At one celebrated event in November 1936 he and Attlee welcomed hunger marchers alongside Wal Harrington, a leading communist and organizer for the unemployed. *Aneurin Bevan*, vol. 1, *1897–1945* (London: McGibbon and Kee, 1962), p. 238.

16 Paynter, *My Generation*, p. 63.

17 William Lawther, who had lost his own brother in Spain, made this pledge in May 1938. A 2s. 6d solidarity levy raised £68,000 of which £50,000 was pledged to help orphaned children.

18 Paynter, *My Generation*, p. 80.

19 For example, *The Times* newspaper, scarcely a radical publication, raised £12,000 in a public appeal. As part of the 'Portraits for Spain scheme', artists were commissioned by wealthy patrons. The Welsh artist Augustus John offered a head-and-shoulders portrait for 500 guineas, an offer taken up by the Cadbury family.

20 For a concise exploration of the doubter's argument see Stradling's *Wales and the Spanish Civil War*, particularly pp. 170–1.

21 Taken from Auden's poem 'Spain 1937'.

4 THE GREAT AND THE GOOD

1 *South Wales Argus*, Monday 12 July 1937.

2 Roy Jenkins (1920–2003), Labour MP, chancellor of the Exchequer, home secretary, president of the European Commission, founder of the Social Democratic Party and distinguished biographer.

3 *South Wales Needs a Plan* (1936). Hilary Marquand (1901–72) was not a natural militant and did not share Nye Bevan's extrovert personality. His permanent secretary, Dame Enid Russell Smith, described him as 'the type of person one might expect to see selling bird seed in a corn merchant's shop'.

4 John Emlyn-Jones had been Liberal MP for North Dorset between 1922 and 1924.

5 The information on John Elwyn Jones comes from an interview with his son Alun in August 2009.

6 Monmouthshire Council Minutes, 29 June 1937, p. 26, Special committee on accommodation for Basque refugees. (In fact fifty children were housed there.)

7 Cyril Cule, 'The Spanish Civil War – a personal viewpoint', typescript memoir, 1975, SUCC SC158.

8 Most of his writing was an assault on the prevailing understanding of events between 1640 and 1660 and an assertion of the revolutionary nature of society during those years.

9 *Western Mail*, 27 July 1937.

10 *Y Cymro*, 9 January 1937, my translation.

11 Cule, 'The Spanish Civil War – a personal viewpoint'.

12 C. Cule, *Spain Unconquered* (Welsh Democratic Union, August 1939).

13 'Y sefyllfa yn Sbaen', *Y Ddraig Goch*, November 1936.

14 G. Thomas, *A Few Selected Exits* (Bridgend: Seren, 1968), p. 102.

15 The number of voluntary teachers from Cardiff University such as Gwyn Thomas who helped out at Cambria House meant the education could be overly academic. This is discussed further in chapter 6.

16 The political achievements of Lord Davies are dealt with more fully by J. Graham Jones in 'The peacemonger', *The Journal of Liberal Democrat History*, 29 (winter 2000/1), 16–23.

17 The best discussion of Bevan's activities on behalf of the Spanish Republic is to be found in Michael Foot's *Aneurin Bevan*, vol. 1, *1897–1945* (London: McGibbon and Kee, 1962).

18 William John Gruffydd, *Y Llenor*, 5, 1 (spring 1936).

5 OUT OF HARM'S WAY

1 Interviews with Alvaro Velasco, Carmarthen, 2007 and 2008.

2 Interview with Paulita Felipe Gomez, Skewen, May 2008.

3 Interview with Josefina Álvarez, February 2008, and Gerado Álvarez, March 2008.

4 Interview with José Armolea, April 2008.

5 G. P. Totoricaguena, *Basque Diaspora: Migration and Transnational Identity* (Reno: University of Nevada Press, 2003), p. 355.

6 J. L. Granja et al., *La España de los nacionalismos y as autonimas* (Madrid: Tecnos, 2001), p. 127.

7 Extract from a radio broadcast by Aguirre, 12 April 1937, cited in *Time Magazine*, 12 April 1937.

8 Interview with Alvaro Velasco, December 2007.

9 Interview with Paula Gomez, May 2008.

10 P. M. Heaton, *Welsh Blockade Runners in the Spanish Civil War* (Newport: Starling Press, 1985).

11 The *España* sank on 30 April 1937, having accidentally struck a Nationalist mine off Santander during the blockade of Bilbao; 854 men drowned.

12 David 'Potato' Jones left St Jean de Luz on 19 April 1937 bound for the port of Alicante. Several writers have drawn attention to the 'coincidence' that the following day new regulations, forbidding traffic in guns were to be imposed.

13 *The Spanish Civil War* documentary series, Granada Television, 1982.

14 Mola's proclamation of 31 March, at the start of the assault on Euzkadi was broadcast on Radio Castilla in Burgos. It was also printed on a leaflet dropped on the main Basque towns.

15 E. Ludendorff, *Die Totale Krieg* [Total War] (Munich, 1934).

16 An award-winning article by George Lowther Steer, in *The Times* on 27 April 1937, brought the massacre to world attention. His 1937 masterpiece, *The Tree of Gernika* (London: Faber, 2009), remains the definitive account of the outrage.

17 Subsequently, on 3 May 1937, Franco denied responsibility for the air raid and claimed that the town had been blown up and then burnt by 'Red Government agents', as a grotesque exercise in misinformation. Even as late as 1967 Luis Bolin, the head of propaganda for Franco, continued to argue that Republicans in Bilbao dispatched Asturian miners to dynamite the town.

18 Audio tape of BBC Radio Wales interview with Paula and Angelita (1987) and interview with Paula in Sketty (May 2008).

19 Ibid.

20 Isabel Fernandez Barrientos in N. Benjamin *Recuerdos: Basque Refugee Children in Great Britain* (Norwich: Mousehold Press, 2007), p. 55.

21 The fields at North Stoneham had been lent by a local farmer, Mr G. H. Brown.

22 Interview with Alvaro Velasco (2008).

23 Paco Robles Hernando, in Benjamin, *Recuerdos*, p. 137.

24 Y. Cloud, *The Basque Children in England* (London: Gollancz, 1937), p. 8. Cloud was the pen name of Yvonne Kapp (1903–99), a political activist and author who worked at the North Stoneham camp. That same year she organized a fund-raising concert for Spain at which Paul Robeson sang and Picasso offered one of his Guernica sketches for sale.

25 Isabel Fernandez Barrientos, in Benjamin, *Recuerdos*, p. 55.

26 J. Fryth, *The Signal was Spain: The Aid Spain Movement in Britain 1936–39* (London: Lawrence and Wishart, 1986), pp. 234–5.

27 Ibid., p. 232.

6 SHELTER FROM THE STORM

1 Interview with Josefina Álvarez, 2008; interview with Paulita Felipe Gomez, Skewen, May 2008. Cambria House is variously described as a former workhouse, infirmary and old people's home. In its time it had probably been all three.

2 *South Wales Argus*, 12 July 1937.

3 Ibid.

4 Ibid.

5 Ibid.

6 An undated typewritten list of names, Basque Children of '37 Association, Oxford.

7 Recording of an interview with Mrs Fernandez (1987), SCC AUD/439.

8 Interview with Paulita Felipe Gomez, Skewen, May 2008, and Gerado Álvarez, March 2008.

9 Recording of an interview with Mrs Fernandez (1987), SCC AUD/439.

10 Interview with Josefina Álvarez; Josefina maintains that Christopher Hill found Mrs Fernandez working in a bar in Cardiff. Other sources say she was living in Caerleon, only yards from Cambria House.

11 Recording of an interview with Angelita (1987), SWC AUD/443.

12 XX (the contributors to the publication were identified only by initials), *Cambria House Journal*, March 1939.

13 Recording of an interview with Angelita (1987), SWC AUD/443. Robeson's words are cited by Hywel Francis in 'Paul Robeson: his legacy for Wales', a talk given in Aberystwyth, 12 July 2003.

14 *Cambria House Journal*, January 1939.

15 A few children were educated outside the home. For example, Gerado went to the local primary school in Caerleon and then on to Abersychan Grammar School.

16 *Cambria House Journal*, April 1939.

17 Interview with Josefina Álvarez, 2008.

18 Interview with Paulita Felipe Gomez, Skewen, May 2008.

19 For example, in December 1938 the children put on concerts in Tredegar, Pontypool, Crumlin and Tonypandy. The following month they were in Treorchy, Penarth, Tylorstown, Pontnewydd and Ton Pentre.

20 *Cambria House Journal*, December 1938.

21 *Cambria House Journal*. The writer of the match report in the *Journal* is most put out that he is listed in the programme as a reserve not a team player. He was appalled to find the same error in newspaper reports the following day. For the sake of posterity let it be recorded that Julio Andres did play right back for the Basque Boys against Moorland Road on 10 May 1939.

22 *Cambria House Journal*, June 1939.

23 Ibid.

24 *Cambria House Journal*, November 1938.

25 *Cambria House Journal*, February 1939.

26 *Cambria House Journal*, August 1939.

27 BA, 'Children and war', *Cambria House Journal*, November 1939.

28 *Cambria House Journal*, February 1939.

29 *Cambria House Journal*, March 1939.

30 C, 'What my parents tell me', *Cambria House Journal*, April 1939.

31 MJA, 'What my mother tells me', *Cambria House Journal*, May 1939.

32 *Cambria House Journal,* February 1939.

33 *Cambria House Journal,* January 1939.

34 'Our new home', *Cambria House Journal,* August 1939.

7 DASTARDLY YARNS

1 *Western Mail,* 19 August 1933. Gareth Jones (1905–35) was a Welsh journalist who exposed the Soviet famine of 1932–3. He was murdered by Chinese bandits.

2 Cited by Richard Binns in *Kite Country* (Rhayader, Powys: self-published, 2005).

3 Interview with Roy James in Brechfa, August 2009.

4 In previous years the camp had been used between March and October by unemployed workers from the valleys engaged on the construction of forestry roads.

5 *Welshman,* 23 July 1937.

6 Minutes of Carmarthenshire Public Assistance Committee, 23 July 1937.

7 Interview with José Armolea, April 2008.

8 *Carmarthen Journal,* 30 July 1937.

9 Ibid.

10 *Welshman,* 30 July 1937.

11 *Carmarthen Journal,* 30 July 1937.

12 Ibid.

13 Interviews with José Armolea, April 2008, and Alvaro Velasco, Carmarthen, 2007.

14 Letter to the *Western Mail,* 28 July 1937.

15 There is contradictory evidence about the number of refugees sent back and their exact destination. In an internal report the NJC said it had, reluctantly, 'parted with eighteen difficult boys who were now in France'. It felt that, 'the reputation of the others should not be jeopardised by the few'. Basque Children Report, NJC, 12 August 1937.

16 Extracts from letters published in the *Carmarthen Journal,* 30 July 1937.

17 Quarterly meeting of Carmarthenshire County Council as reported in the *Welshman,* 30 July 1937.

18 Councillor J. Llewelyn Evans of Llanelli, in reply to Alderman H.V. Watkins of Llandovery, Tuesday 22 July 1937.

19 *Western Mail*, 25 May 1937.

20 Interview with José Armolea, April 2008.

21 The family of Charlie Jones of 12 Little Water Street, Carmarthen.

22 Interview with Alvaro Velasco, 2008.

23 These were Mrs Tong, née Sinda Villulas, and Mr Zamora, the father of Frank who fought and died for the International Brigade, cited by G. Eaton, *Neath and the Spanish Civil War* (Neath: privately published, 1980), p. 73.

24 Ibid.

25 R. Evans, 'Onllwyn Teifi Parish History'. Typewritten manuscript, 110. Bronwydd Mansion was used as a Jewish boarding school during the Second World War. After the war it was stripped of its fittings. It was destroyed by fire in the 1980s.

26 H. Thomas, *The Spanish Civil War* (Harmondsworth: Penguin, 1974), p. 573.

27 D. Legarretta, *The Guernica Generation: Basque Refugee Children of the Spanish Civil War* (Reno: Unviersity of Nevada Press, 1984), chapter 3, pp. 99–134.

28 *Scarborough Evening News*, 15 July 1937.

29 *Hansard*, 28 July 1937, vol. 326, cc 2126 7W.

30 *Sunday Dispatch*, 25 July 1937; *Daily Mail*, 26 July 1937, The children were described amongst other things as, 'dangerous Reds' and 'Christ hating little Communists'. The headline in the *Catholic Times* on 30 July was: 'These Basque babies are Red terrors'.

31 *South Wales Argus*, 10 August 1937; the headline was 'Basque children bogey'.

32 Basque Children's Committee minutes, 31 August 1937.

33 Basque Refugee Children, *New Statesman and Nation*, 21 August 1937.

34 'Basque children, the stark truth', *John Bull*, August 1937.

35 *Bulletin of the NJCSR*, March 1938. Among the contributions recorded were: Band of Hope: £32, Amalgamated Society of Woodworkers: £5, YMCA: £2 2s.

36 *Llanelly and County Guardian*, 8 July 1937.

37 *Llanelly and County Guardian*, 29 July 1937.

38 Ibid. The mayor, despite his political objections, made a donation of £35 from his own pocket.

39 *Llanelly and County Guardian*, 26 August 1937.

8 A TIDAL WAVE OF GIVING

1 The story of Antonia and Lola is based on interviews carried out by correspondence in 2008. The help of Antonia's son Pedro was invaluable.

2 Extracts from D. Eizaguirre (ed.), *Corazón de Cartón* (self-published, 1999), featuring recollections from Maria Luisa Fuentas, Amelia Fuentas and Begona Ballesteros, pp. 130–1 and 144–5.

3 Sketty Park House was demolished in 1973. All that remains is a gothic folly, the belvedere.

4 Eizaguirre (ed.), *Corazón de Cartón*, pp. 130–1.

5 *South Wales Evening Post*, 5 July 1937.

6 *South Wales Evening Post*, 3 July 1937.

7 Appeal from the mayor of Swansea, 2 July 1937.

8 Interview with Mrs Steel (formerly Rose Noriega), SWCC – vid/32.

9 *South Wales Evening Post*, 2 August 1983.

10 Interview with Mrs Steel (formerly Rose Noriega), SWCC – vid/32.

11 Eizaguirre (ed.), *Corazón de Cartón*, pp. 130–1.

12 Ibid.

13 D. Ivor Saunders, the borough chartered surveyor, is the man who did most to ensure the success of the Swansea project. His family 'adopted' a Basque girl, Aurelia Mesones, until her return to her parents in January 1938.

14 The contents of the visitors' box for one week in July 1937 came to £1 5s. 3d.

15 G. Eaton, *Neath and the Spanish Civil War* (Neath: privately published, 1980), pp. 66–73.

16 *South Wales Evening Post*, 19 July 1937.

17 L. Santamaria, *Agur Euskadi, hasta nunca* (Madrid: Ministerio de Trabajo e Inmigracion, 2008). Chapter 5 of this book, written in Spanish, gives a personal account of the author's time in Swansea.

18 *South Wales Evening Post*, 19 July 1937. Among these, according to published lists of donors, was Mr Zamara of Abercraf and Mrs Cuesto and Mr Phozano of Dowlais.

19 After this prod, the town's Chamber of Trade did agree to a one off contribution of ten guineas.

20 Correspondence from Tini's son Terry Dineen with the Basque Children of '37 Association (2006).

21 Antonia remembers a teacher and an auxiliary returning to Spain. The teacher had been particularly strict with the children: 'Unfortunately, she possessed a large nose and because of this the kids referred to her, amongst themselves, as the Parrot.'

9 'THE BEST PART OF MY LIFE'

1 'The week's look round by Observer', *The Pioneer*, 30 May 1937.

2 In a little over a month a house had been secured and a general committee with a membership of twenty-one was formed on 10 July 1937.

3 John Williams-Hughes, the joint-secretary of the Spanish Medical Aid Committee in Wales, was a writer and journalist from Marianglas on Anglesey. He worked in Madrid for the Red Cross and on his return from Spain he toured the country, speaking at meetings, giving broadcasts and writing articles.

4 North Wales Basque Children's Home appeal, August 1937.

5 *Pioneer*, 28 April 1938.

6 These accusations, made much later by Douglas Hyde, are discussed below. He described the committee as 'the broadest and most Popular–Front-ish yet'. D. Hyde, *I Believed: The Autobiography of a Former British Communist* (London: The Reprint Society, 1952), p. 63.

7 Private letter from J. Wesley Jones to Douglas Hyde, 18 August 1937, private collection, RL.

8 'The week's look round by Observer', *North Wales Pioneer*, 2 July 1937.

9 *North Wales Weekly News*, 26 July 1937.

10 Private letter from J. Wesley Jones to Douglas Hyde, 13 August 1937, RL.

11 *North Wales Weekly News*, 5 August 1937.

12 *North Wales Pioneer*, 12 August 1937.

13 *North Wales Weekly News*, 5 August, 1937.

14 Ibid.

15 Internal treasurer's report, August 1937, RL.

16 Private letter from J. Wesley Jones to Douglas Hyde, 5 September 1937.

17 *North Wales Pioneer*, 27 January 1938.

18 *North Wales Pioneer*, 28 April 1938.

19 *North Wales Pioneer*, 22 September 1938.

20 Appeal for donations of furniture, *North Wales Pioneer*, 2 July 1937.

21 *North Wales Weekly News*, 5 August 1937.

22 *North Wales Weekly News*, 5 September 1937.

23 *North Wales Pioneer*, 22 September 1938.

24 *North Wales Pioneer*, 27 October 1938.

25 *North Wales Pioneer*, 28 April 1938.

26 *North Wales Weekly News*, 5 May 2005.

27 'The week's look round by Observer', *North Wales Pioneer*, 2 July 1937.

28 Just before he died in 1996 he described himself on his hospital forms as an agnostic Christian, *Independent*, 26 September 1996.

29 Hyde, *I Believed*, p. 58.

30 *Wrexham Leader*, 9 April 1937.

31 Hyde, *I Believed*, p. 59.

32 *Caernarvon and Denbigh Herald*, 9 April 1937.

33 J. Pugh, *A Most Expensive Prisoner: Tom Jones, Rhosllannerchrugog's Biography* (Llanrwst: Gwasg Carreg Gwalch,1988), p. 45.

34 D. Hyde, *Dedication and Leadership: Learning from the Communists* (Chicago: University of Notre Dame Press, 1956), p. 97.

35 The meetings were on 6 April in Caernarfon and 9 March in Wrexham.

36 Letter from Señor José de Lisaro, the Basque government delegate to London, to the secretary of the Old Colwyn Children's home, *North Wales Pioneer*, 2 June 1938.

37 *North Wales Weekly News*, 5 August 1937.

10 FAULT LINES

1 *South Wales Argus*, 8 July 1937.

2 *Catholic Times*, 25 June 1937. Repeated enquiries to the Sisters of Nazareth archive in Hammersmith have failed to elicit further details or even to confirm absolutely the existence of such a home.

3 *North Wales Weekly News,* 22 July 1937.

4 Spokesman for US Catholic hierarchy quoted in *Time Magazine,* 31 May 1937.

5 *Daily Worker,* 16 August 1937.

6 Cited in H. Thomas, *The Spanish Civil War* (Harmondsworth: Penguin, 1973), p. 575. Although solidly pro-Franco, Hinsley was a noted foe of Italian and German totalitarianism. He had condemned Mussolini's invasion of Abyssinia and called the Nazis a 'pagan clique of upstart tyrants'.

7 April 1938, radio broadcast to the Spanish faithful by Pius XII.

8 *Catholic Times,* 30 May.

9 Mr Golden of the Save the Children Fund wrote to the Foreign Office to say that he 'would sooner see them die in their own land than rot slowly in exile'. Cited in A. Bell, *Only for Three Months: The Basque Children in Exile* (Norwich: Mousehold Press, 1996), p. 29.

10 *Daily Mail,* Editorial, 1 July 1937.

11 Letter to *The Times,* 2 June 1937, claimed the disease was well known to be 'ravaging northern Spain'.

12 The National Joint Committee for Spanish Refugees (NJCSP) (March 1938) accused Wilson and his committee of conducting a 'wicked campaign' of deliberate misrepresentation and maintained that 'intrigues against the children' were preventing humanitarian aid.

13 Report of a speech by Sir Nairne Stewart-Sanderson in the *Manchester Guardian* cited in *Spanish Relief,* the bulletin of the NJCSP, March 1938.

14 Luis Bolin, a former London correspondent of the *ABC* newspaper, was Franco's press director, responsible for arranging for sympathetic war correspondents to make tours of the battle areas.

15 *Western Mail,* 26 September 1938.

16 *Time Magazine,* 30 May 1938.

17 Thomas, *The Spanish Civil War,* pp. 588–91. See also Alun Menai Williams's account of his time in the International Brigade, *From the Rhondda to the Ebro* (Pontypool: Warren and Pell, 2004), published shortly before his death.

18 *Y Ddraig Goch,* 63 (September 1938). Bebb concluded his piece by saying: 'we extend our condolences to Spain, to both armies'.

19 'Esbonio Helynt Sbaen', *Y Ddraig Goch,* 39 (September 1936).

20 D. J. Davies of Ammanford, a leading member of Plaid Cymru from its inception, epitomizes this internationalist and leftist strand within the party, as does Walter Dowding of Brynmawr.

21 The most detailed discussion of the genesis of the party and the destruction of the bombing school is to be found in D. H. Davies, *The Welsh Nationalist Party, 1925–45: A Call to Nationhood* (Cardiff: University of Wales Press, 1983).

22 *Western Mail*, 26 October 1936.

23 The poem 'Cerddi'r Gaeaf' (1952) by R.Williams Parry is one indication of the almost mythical status that Penyberth attained amongst Welsh speakers.

24 *South Wales Argus*, 12 August 1937.

11 DON'T SING THE SONGS OF THE PAST

1 *Cambria House Journal*, May 1939.

2 L. Abse, *Private Member* (London: MacDonald, 1973), pp. 38–40.

3 The Museu Memorial de l'Exili at La Junquera is an invaluable archive dedicated to the memory of the exile.

4 Recording of Maria Fernandez (1987), AUD/439, SCC.

5 *Cambria House Journal*, June 1939.

6 *Cambria House Journal*, November 1939.

7 'A Message to all our friends by Jack Williams', *Cambria House Journal*, November 1939.

8 Interview with Maria Fernandez, SWC AUD 439.

9 Figures cited in K. Ericsson and E. Simonsen (eds), *Children of World War II: The Hidden Enemy Legacy* (New York: Berg, 2005), pp. 115–38. Chapter 6, by Michael Richards, deals with the ideology and psychology of the war children in Franco's Spain.

10 Taken from an interview with Franco by Manuel Aznar, *Spain* magazine, 26 January 1939.

11 Ericsson and Simonsen (eds), *Children of World War II*.

12 Paul McGuire, article in the *Catholic Herald*, cited by Judith Keane in *Fighting for Franco* (2001).

13 Maria Luisa Fuentes (1999), in D. Eizaguirre (ed.), *Corazón de Cartón* (self-published, 1999), pp. 144–5.

14 *Cambria House Journal*, November 1939.

15 After Franco's victory the campaign of the south Wales miners took on a more clandestine aspect, giving aid to Spanish Republicans on the run. These

usually arrived by tramp steamer where they were helped by a local character called Meth Jones. At one point there were five stowaways being accommodated in a house in Penarth at the expense of the Fed. See W. Paynter, *My Generation* (London: Allen and Unwin, 1973), p. 80.

16 There were regular appeals for donations to pay the cost of transit to the Latin American republics of those for whom return to Spain 'might mean instant death'. David L. Wickes, the organizer for south Wales for Spanish Relief used Cambria House as the address for an appeal to help evacuate the '40,000 victims of the Spanish War to South America' (*Cambria House Journal*, August 1939).

17 *Cambria House Journal*, September 1939.

12 NOT OURS BUT OURS TO LOOK AFTER

1 Taken from conversations with Alvaro Velasco in Carmarthen during 2006–8.

2 C. Cule, 'The Spanish Civil War: a personal viewpoint', typescript memoir, 1975, SUCC SC158.

3 Interview with Josefina Álvarez, February 2008.

4 K. Frank, *Indira* (Orlando, FL: Houghton Mifflin, 2002).

5 *Cambria House Journal*, January 1939.

6 *Cambria House Journal*, August 1939.

7 Sonia Fisher, the daughter of George Phillips, cited on *caerleon.net/archive*.

8 Maria Carmen de Andres Elorriaga, in N. Benjamin, *Recuerdos: Basque Refugee Children in Great Britain* (Norwich: Mousehold Press, 2007), pp. 9–14.

9 Interview with Paula Gomez, May 2008.

10 Cule, 'The Spanish Civil War'.

11 Ibid.

12 Obituary in the *Guardian*, 23 April 2002. Cyril Cule's books are *Cymro Grwydr*, about his travels, and a novel, *Gweld y Byd*.

13 *North Wales Pioneer*, 15 December 1938.

14 Interview with José Armolea, April 2008.

15 Isabel Barreintos in Benjamin, *Recuerdos*, p. 55.

16 P. Cope, *Wise and Foolish Dreamers* (Cardiff: Welsh Centre for International Affairs, 2007), pp. 57–8.

17 Interview with Paula Gomez, May 2008.

18 Interview with Josefina Álvarez, February 2008.

19 'A family's fond adios to Maria', *South Wales Argus*, 1 February 2001.

20 Interview with Mrs Fernandez (1987) 16, AUD/439, recording of Maria Fernandez, SCC.

21 Ibid.

22 *Spanish Relief*, NJC bulletin, 15 (September 1938).

BIBLIOGRAPHY

INTERVIEWS CONDUCTED IN 2008 AND 2009

Gerado Álvarez
José Armolea
Paula Felipe
Roy James
Alun Emlyn Jones
Pedro Perez
Josefina Savery, née Álvarez
Alvaro Velasco

AUDIO-TAPED INTERVIEWS (ALL SWCC)

Abercraf Community Study, AUD 2000
Angelita Gomez, AD/443
Maria Fernandez, AUD/439
Spanish Immigrants in Abercraf, AUD/263
Will Paynter, AUD/287
Mrs Steel, VID/32

PRIMARY COLLECTIONS

Basque Children of '37 Archive, Oxford
Conwy Archive Service, Llandudno

National Newspaper Archive, Colindale, London
Rosemary Logan private collection, London (RL)
Swansea University Coalfield Collection (SUCC)
South Wales Miners' Library, Hendrefoilan, Swansea (SWML)
West Glamorgan Archive Service, Swansea

NEWSPAPERS AND JOURNALS

Caernarvon and Denbigh Herald
Catholic Times
Daily Mail
Daily Worker
John Bull
Llanelly and County Guardian
Manchester Guardian
New Statesman and Nation
New York Herald Tribune
North Wales Pioneer
North Wales Weekly News
Scarborough Evening News
South Wales Argus
South Wales Echo
Time Magazine
Welshman
Western Mail
The Welsh Review
Wrexham Leader
Y Cymro
Y Ddraig Goch
Y Llenor

SECONDARY WORKS

Abse, L., *Private Member* (London: MacDonald, 1973).
Beevor, A., *The Battle for Spain: the Spanish Civil War* (London: Weidenfeld and Nicolson, 2006).
Bell, A., *Only for Three Months: The Basque Children in Exile* (Norwich: Mousehold Press, 1996).
Benjamin, N., *Recuerdos: Basque Refugee Children in Great Britain* (Norwich: Mousehold Press, 2007).
Buchanan, T., *The British Labour Movement and the Spanish Civil War* (Cambridge: Cambridge University Press, 1992).
Calvert, A., *Impressions of Spain* (London: Philip and Son, 1903).

Clark, R. P., *The Basques, the Franco Years and Beyond* (Reno: University of Nevada Press, 1979).
Cloud, Y., *The Basque Children in England* (London: Gollancz, 1937).
Cope, P., *Wise and Foolish Dreamers* (Cardiff: Welsh Centre for International Affairs, 2007).
Cule, C., *Spain Unconquered* (Newport: Welsh Democratic Union, 1937).
——, 'The Spanish Civil War – a personal viewpoint', typescript memoir, 1975, SUCC SC158.
Davies, D. H., *The Welsh Nationalist Party, 1925–45: A Call to Nationhood* (Cardiff: University of Wales Press, 1983).
Davies, W. H., 'Alvaro's Story', *Carmarthenshire Life*, August 2006.
Davies, J., *A History of Wales* (Harmondsworth: Penguin, 2006).
Eaton, G., *Neath and the Spanish Civil War* (Neath: privately published, 1980).
Eizaguirre, D. (ed.), *Corazón de Cartón* (self-published, 1999).
Ericsson, K. and E. Simonsen (eds), *Children of World War II: The Hidden Enemy Legacy* (New York: Berg, 2005).
Evans, D. G., *A History of Wales, 1906–2000* (Cardiff: University of Wales Press, 2000).
Evans, R., 'Onllwyn Teifi parish history', typewritten manuscript, ADX/870, Ceredigion Archives, Aberystwyth, 2006.
Foot, M., *Aneurin Bevan*, vol. 1, *1897–1945* (London: MacGibbon and Kee, 1962).
Francis, H., *Miners Against Fascism: Wales and the Spanish Civil War* (London: Lawrence and Wishart, 1984).
—— and D. Smith, *The Fed: A History of South Wales Miners in the Twentieth Century* (London: Lawrence and Wishart, 1980).
Frank, K., *Indira* (Orlando, FL: Houghton Mifflin, 2002).
Fryth, J., *The Signal was Spain: The Aid Spain Movement in Britain 1936–39* (London: Lawrence and Wishart, 1986).
Garratt, G. T., *Mussolini's Roman Empire* (Harmondsworth: Penguin, 1937).
Giles, G., 'From Bilbao to Caerleon', *Gwent Local History Journal*, 98 (spring 2005).
Granja, J. L. et al., *La España de los nacionalismos y as autonima* (Madrid: Tecnos, 2001).
Heaton, P. M., *Welsh Blockade Runners in the Spanish Civil War* (Newport: Starling Press, 1985).
Hooper, J., *The New Spaniards* (Harmondsworth: Penguin, 2006).
Hyde , D., *I Believed: The Autobiography of a Former British Communist* (London: The Reprint Society, 1952).
——, *Dedication and Leadership: Learning from the Communists* (Chicago: University of Notre Dame Press, 1956).
Jenkins, I., *Idris Davies of Rhymney: A Personal Memoir* (Llandysul: Gwasg Gomer, 1986).
Jones, L., *We Live* ([1937] London: Lawrence and Wishart, 1978).
Keane, J., *Fighting for Franco: International Volunteers in Nationalist Spain* (Leicester: Leicester University Press, 2001).

Kleine-Ahlbrandt, W. M., *The Policy of Simmering* (The Hague: Martinus Nijhoff, 1962).

Kushner, T. and K. Knox, *Refugees in an Age of Genocide* (London: Routledge, 2001).

Kurlansky, M., *The Basque History of the World* (London: Vintage, 2000).

Lagretta, D., *The Guernica Generation: Basque Refugee Children of the Spanish Civil War* (Reno: University of Nevada Press, 1984).

Ludendorff, E., *Die Totale Krieg* [Total War] (Munich, 1934).

Mates, L., 'A most fruitful period? The north-east and the Popular Front period, 1935–39', *North East History*, 36 (2004), 54–98.

Morgan, K. O., *Rebirth of a Nation: A History of Modern Wales* (Oxford: Oxford University Press, 1981).

Morris, J., *The Matter of Wales: Epic Views of a Small Country* (Harmondsworth: Penguin, 1984).

Nicholson, H., *Diaries and Letters* (London: Faber, 1968).

Paynter, W., *My Generation* (London: Allen and Unwin, 1972).

Pugh, J., *A Most Expensive Prisoner: Tom Jones, Rhosllannerchrugog's Biography* (Llanrwst: Gwasg Carreg Gwalch, 1988).

Santamaria, L., *Agur Euskadi, hasta nunca* (Madrid: Ministerio de Trabajo e Inmigracion, 2008).

Sinclair, N. M. C., *The Tiger Bay Story* (Cardiff: Butetown History & Arts Project, 1993).

Steer, G. L., *The Tree of Guernika* ([1938] London: Faber, 2009).

Stradling, R., *Cardiff and the Spanish Civil War* (Cardiff: Butetown History and Arts Project, 1996).

——, *Wales and the Spanish Civil War: The Dragon's Dearest Cause?* (Cardiff: University of Wales Press, 2004).

——, 'A fine romance', *Planet*, 196 (autumn 2009), 77–83.

Thomas, G., *A Few Selected Exits* (Bridgend: Seren Books, 1994).

Thomas, H., *The Spanish Civil War* (Harmondsworth: Penguin, 1973).

Thomas, M., 'Not unlike Bilbao', *Planet*, 192 (December/January 2008/2009), 68–74.

Totoricaguena, G. P., *Basque Diaspora: Migration and Transnational Identity* (Reno: University of Nevada Press, 2003).

Williams, A. M. , *From the Rhondda to the Ebro* (Pontypool: Warren and Pell, 2004).

Williams, G. A., *The Welsh in their History* (London: Croom Helm, 1982).

——, *When was Wales?: A History of the Welsh* (Harmondsworth: Penguin, 1985).

INDEX